HOLY
INADEQUATE

Andrew H Rea

First published in Great Britain by L.R. Price Publications Ltd, 2020.

This edition published by:
L.R. Price Publications Ltd.
27 Old Gloucester Street,
London, WC1N 3AX.
www.lrpricepublications.com

Copyright © 2020.

The right of Andrew H Rea to be identified as author of this work has been asserted in accordance with sections 77 and 78 of the Copyright, Designs and Patents Act, 1988.

Cover Design courtesy of Carolyn Rea
Limited licence provided to L.R. Price Publications Ltd..
Copyright © Carolyn Rea, 2020.
Carolyn Rea Graphic Design
www.carolynrea.com

This book is protected by copyright under the Berne Convention.
No reproduction without permission.

ISBN13: 9781838061005

HOLY
INADEQUATE

Andrew H Rea

CHAPTER ONE
In the Beginning

It was a Sunday afternoon in 2015. My wife Jean and I were sitting in the lounge of our house, in La Marina, a large urbanization near Torrevieja, Spain. We had moved permanently from the U.K. in July 2012, and I had Permission to Officiate (PTO) from the Anglican Diocese of Europe, as an associate priest, in the Chaplaincy of St. Peter and St. Paul, Torrevieja.

We had just returned from my conducting a service in one of the Chaplaincy congregations – one of several English-speaking congregations, who mainly rent churches owned by the Roman Catholic Church. It was now time for lunch and a rest. At nearly seventy years of age, the mind is still active but the body needs rest!

That was when I remember feeling a strange experience, which I have, over the years, come to recognize: *He's at it again; here it comes...*

The message was clear and uncomplicated: I was to start a Christian retreat centre.

As I reflected on this, I turned to Jean: "Got a call to start a retreat."

As always, she was supportive. There were no exclamations of: "What?! Are you mad?! We're settled here and have a good life." Though, such a reaction would have been justified.

I got out of my chair and paced the small room, my mind racing.

"This will be the biggest rollercoaster ride we have ever been on," I said. "And, at our age."

Words tumbled out, as I started to think of the enormity of the complications involved. We would need to sell our house, which we had just got the way we wanted. Could we afford all the costs? Where on Earth would we find somewhere to start a retreat? Jean is a very good listener, thank God.

I often think of the people God calls - the big guys: Abraham, Moses, Saul... I have never been a maintainer - a man who can do the same duties week in and week out. People like that are utterly necessary, and in a way I admire them: men and women who are called to ministry and get on with it.

I worked in child protection for forty years, first as a probation officer, then in child protection, and latterly as a children's guardian - representing children in care proceedings, and overseeing the work of social workers on their behalf. I would advise judges on how appropriate court orders were to help the children. So, how did I get into religion, and how did it fit in with my secular work? Very well, as it turned out.

I decided early on that being a maintainer was not for me; if I was to be ordained, then there would need to be challenges outside of the daily routine. Ordination was always at the back of my mind, but I tried not to think too much about it. I had an active lay-ministry, and along with my care work, found this a satisfying combination.

As a nine-year-old, I remember wearing a second-hand, lovat-green dressing gown, with my pyjama jacket back to front, as I danced around the house, pretending to be a vicar - much to the amusement of my parents. Mum always knew my calling. When I called her at the age of thirty-odd, asking if she knew where my baptism certificate might be, her comment was: "Ah, I know why you want that."

My father was a journalist and we moved about England a great deal. I went to five grammar schools and several primary schools, which certainly didn't help my education: every new grammar school I started at was usually ahead of my previous school. When I was studying for my

G.C.E. exams they put me in "5 Woodwork", because I was useless for "5 Latin" or "5 Express" - the latter would become doctors, barristers and leaders. Even "5 Spanish" was a no-hoper. Because I was so far behind, they made me stay an extra year in 5 Woodwork.

I was useless at woodwork; no practical ability, whatsoever. The only thing I really remember about it is the teacher, "Basher" Wooton - so named because he would hit his useless pupils with a big piece of wood - at one of the grammar schools. He would say: "Ee, lad, you can take it off, but you can't put it back on!" Funny, but that has been one of my guiding rules in life – thanks, Basher.

Dad was an agnostic. He wanted to be convinced, with many a doubt – this is not unusual. He was an emotionally-damaged man, his father - who I never met - a nasty alcoholic. My grandfather was also a journalist, who started a successful public relations company (which he allegedly sold for ten bob, in a pub, one night). His wife would spend hours chasing ambulances and fire engines, to get a story for him, whilst buying furniture for their home, which he would often smash up, in a drunken rage. Dad told me he ended up in digs at the age of twelve, which he had to leave on Christmas Day, so his landlady could celebrate Christmas with her family. Walking the streets, with cardboard in the soles of his worn shoes, I understand how he became an expert on films and film stars: he spent so much lonely time in dark, but warm, cinemas.

He started working as a junior reporter, on a weekly newspaper in his hometown, gaining his first editorship at the age of twenty-eight. After eight successful years there he travelled the country, with my mother and I, spending a few weeks here; a few weeks there. The shortest period of settlement I remember, in my early teens, was just one week; he started work as a sub-editor on the Monday, and I think he actually resigned on the day he started, leaving on the Friday. This meant another move to rented accommodation, and another change of school for me.

I remember, at my third grammar school, often throwing up my school dinner in the corridor, and being terrified of getting a bus "home", instead walking fifteen miles; I've not many happy childhood memories.

One amusing episode stands out a few years later, of when my parents came to visit me one day, and Dad and I went for a walk. I was twenty-three, just married and with a baby daughter. I had hair halfway down my back, and a bushy beard (I've still got the beard, though not bushy, and very little hair!), prompting my dad to exclaim: "I know you believe in Jesus Christ, but do you have to go round looking like Him?"

Mum had a miserable life. She had previously married an apparently kind and gentle man, before the second world war came along; she was living with her parents, when the dreaded, black-edged telegram arrived: her husband had been blown up. The coffin arrived with a note attached: "Please do not open this coffin." Her first son had just been born, and Mum told me that he laughed as she opened the telegram. In 1946, she remarried, mainly to get away from her mother, who treated her like a skivvy. *Bad decision, Mum; bad choice.* I was born in 1947.

Wherever we three lived, in rented accommodation (my half-brother had by now left home), Mum would always take me to a local church on Sunday evening. Usually low church - no bells and smells; known as evangelical, in the Anglican tradition.

I was *called* on Christmas Day, at the age of nine.

My parents had bought a grocery shop, and Mum ran it, whilst Dad worked as editor of a weekly newspaper (this was during his eight-year career "success"). Early on Christmas morning, I crept down the cold, dark staircase, opened the lounge door and felt for the light switch. As the dim light appeared (electricity costs money) I hoped to see toys and/or games, wrapped in Christmas paper. To my great disappointment, all I saw was a pile of books: samples my father received, in his job.

My eyes fell on one of the books: a Bible – *Mum, again*.

I thumbed disconsolately through its pages, and it opened at "John 6; verse 35":

"Jesus said to them, 'I am the bread of life. Whoever comes to me will never be hungry, and whoever believes in me will never be thirsty'."

It pierced my young soul, for eternity. That was when I started dressing up as a vicar, though it would take me almost five decades to gain ordination in the Church of England.

CHAPTER TWO

The In-Between Years...

Early Career

I had a chequered career start, though was pretty successful in worldly terms.

I only achieved four G.C.E.s at the first attempt: English Language, English Literature, Maths and - to my father's great annoyance - Religious Education (achieving next to top grade in this subject). When the results arrived, we were living in a rented house in Dewsbury. I was dreading telling the old man.

"Religious Education! What the bloody hell good is Religious Education?"

He got me a job, as a trainee reporter, on the weekly newspaper where he was deputy-editor. Mum saw the dangers of this: Dad falls out with the editor (again) and gets the sack, or, more likely, just moves on, and Andrew is left without a job. So, one Saturday afternoon, Mum and I were walking around Leeds, when she pushed me into a branch of Woolworth's, telling me to ask for the manager, and say that I wanted to be his trainee manager. I left the store minutes later, mission accomplished.

On the Monday morning I arrived at the store, smartly dressed in my best dark-grey suit (my one and only), a white shirt, with separate starched collar and my old school tie. The manager leant across the top of his desk and nearly wet himself with laughter – the only time I ever saw him laugh, in my brief encounter with store management. He was a miserable man, with a camp-bed in the corner of his office, on which he spent most of his nights.

"Just look at you! Do you think you're a floor-walker, already? If you come back tomorrow, wear jeans and a T-shirt: you're starting on the loading bay." I didn't possess a pair of jeans, but I had some old trousers.

I did a day or two on the loading bay, fell off the back of a lorry and ended up in hospital, with slipped discs; I spent six weeks in plaster, from my neck to my waist.

Dad seemed to experience a moment of understanding, and suggested that I return to school, to do an A-level course, and live with my maternal grandparents (which I did, for much of my teenage life).

I managed one year of A-levels, before I saw an advertisement for bank work - I applied because I needed money. Dad (who was by now in the seaside hotel trade, as Mum did all the cooking - three times a day, plus suppers) wasn't any help.

I got the job, though only after much hassle between my father and the bank concerned: their advertisement had read "local bank", but it turned out that they wanted me to start at one of their large town branches, twenty miles away. Dad won the argument, and I arrived to start at the local branch on Monday morning, wearing my best grey suit. This time, I wasn't told to go home and change into my scruffs, although the job did entail carrying heavy, leather-bound ledgers out of the strong room, returning them at night, making cups of tea and stoking the boiler. However, I did deal with customers, over a large counter with no security grilles – face-to-face stuff, which included working on Saturday mornings.

Every customer was to be paid out in brand-new banknotes - nothing used, and one of the few things I learnt, in my fifteen months of utter boredom, was how to count banknotes quickly. That, and how to use an ancient posting machine, to type in customers' account details. It kept breaking down, and over a cup of tea one day, I got talking to the company's mechanic, on one of his regular visits to the branch. Why didn't I apply to be a trainee mechanic? he enquired. *Good idea, thanks.*

So, I applied to the company and was sent for a medical, with a weird doctor. He asked me to supply a urine sample, and told me not to shake off afterwards, as the drops could carry for twenty feet. Reminded me of the days at junior school, when we boys would stand in a line in the bogs, to see who could pee the farthest up the wall. I didn't get offered a job with the company, but I did see an advertisement in the internal bank mail, recruiting computer programmers. *Yes!*

I had failed my banking exams, after attending night school for an age, and my banking career was rapidly coming to an end. So, the bank sent me to test for the new role - it appeared that my brain is not suited to computers. Subsequent years have borne out this knowledge, so no complaints there.

One Sunday afternoon, I went for a drive with three friends - two girls and a boy - to the Lake District. We were in a Triumph Herald, owned by the other lad. We arrived in a small village, where we got split up.

I saw a little church, which I felt I must enter. As I stood in the aisle, I saw a wonderful bright light, in front of the altar – it reminded me of the disciples' experience, at the Transfiguration. Was it Jesus? Was it an angel? I was completely overwhelmed, and still I cannot explain it. I felt so loved, so peaceful, that I wanted to stay there forever. I must have eventually left the church and found my friends, but I was struck dumb for the whole return journey; I couldn't say a word, for the rest of the day.

I look back on that beautiful experience and have no explanation, other than that it definitely happened. A glimpse of Heaven, gifted to encourage me - that is all I can surmise, in trying to describe the unexplainable; a spiritual meeting, with no words necessary. If that is what Heaven is like - if that is being in the presence of Almighty God - then Heaven is beyond anything imaginable.

Back to reality - with a bang! The bank wanted me at another branch, and the reason soon became clear: I was superfluous at this small branch.

During my brief banking career, I had become friends with another junior. He had a Velocette Venom motorcycle, which I much admired - and a girlfriend, who competed in beauty contests! I, myself, was transported by the spinster chief cashier, in her spotless A40. Every morning she would wait for me at an arranged spot, and I was always late - her twitchy fingers would fiddle on the steering wheel, as she gave me her daily lecture about good timekeeping.

So, I bought a 1955, 350cc Matchless motorbike, which I enjoyed riding to and from work. Then, I bought an old Bond three-wheeler - my first car! My new friend - the other junior - asked to take it for a spin one day, and managed to turn it over after hitting a kerb, smashing the windscreen. My dad went to see his dad, but got nowhere – I suspect that was a fiery meeting, not affording opportunities to politely request compensation.

I had to get out of banking! Preferably into something interesting.

I saw an advertisement for a trainee sales representative, with Cadbury Bros. Ltd. *Yes!* I was interviewed by the sales director, who asked me to sell him his own fountain pen. I impressed him; he said that they had never put anyone on the road at the age of nineteen, but I was offered the job and did my training at Bourneville.

I could write a book on my exploits there! Part of my training involved working in the factory, so I understood how those famous goods

I was to sell were produced. At the time, a potato powder called "Smash" was being developed, which only needed mixing with hot water to make mashed potato. When I hit the road as a rep, Smash became part of my daily diet, as well as chocolate biscuits, which were supplied by another trainee rep, with whom I shared a rented bungalow. I was to sell chocolate, while he sold Smash and biscuits as a grocery rep. We would have a half-pound Dairy Milk chocolate bar for dessert.

Whilst at Bourneville, I was sent to an upper floor of the factory, with another trainee rep, where we were told how to mix the ingredients for Smash. When satisfied, we were to open a chute to the floor below, where a machine would pour it into packets. On our first day - possibly after a hard night's partying - we forgot how much potato powder we had mixed in with the other necessary ingredients: milk powder and salt. When a member of the Cadbury family appeared - in his blue factory jacket, striped with grey, and a cap to match - to ask how we were progressing, we mumbled: "Very well, thanks," whilst hoping that he wouldn't go downstairs to sample our mixture.

Great fun, those days of Matthew and Son, and Cat Stephens (as he was then known). I had a company car, and was driving all over the north of England, doing relief work. Chocolate samples, galore! My weight increased, substantially. My total number of crashes in company vehicles was five - though no injuries, thank goodness. After three bumps, they made me pay the insurance excess.

After three years, and two sales territories of my own, my sales manager called me into his office one day. He asked if sales was really my forte, as he pushed a piece of paper and a biro across his desk, for my resignation. That was fine: I had already secured a job by then, as Tele-Ad Sales Manager, on an evening newspaper, in York (would I never get newspapers out of my blood?).

I wrote a weekly motoring article called: "Talking Cars, by Andy Rea", and produced other articles. At only twenty-three, my career was on the up; at last, I had arrived.

It was at this point that my desire to write took off. I became involved with the Arts Centre in York, where I was intoxicated by drama, and all the things which go with it. I even tried my hand at acting, prancing around the floor, like a nymph possessed. My acting skills were challenged, when I came face to face with a local solicitor, who stared into my eyes and spat his rehearsal lines into my face. Honed to the point at which I doubted "up front" to be my forte, I decided that scriptwriting was more my thing.

I wrote a stage play, entitled *Turpin Hero* – well, I was in York, and Dick had been a famous highwayman. It was a sort of comedy, including an over-the-fence conversation about Mr. Turpin's exploits, by two buxom ladies, with Northern accents. I was to play the lead, and I easily got into exploring an unfurnished stage, with the actors attired in matching, black outfits – but, a few days before the opening night, I bottled it, completely. I persuaded a friend in the company to take over, and reiterated that my forte was writing – and possibly producing and directing; certainly not up front, under the spots.

The production was mentioned in a national newspaper, and I heard that the actor Alan Bates was interested in purchasing the manuscript, and producing it on a national basis. Nothing came of this highlight, but it boosted my confidence in my artistic ability. Over the following decade, I wrote several half-hour television comedies in my spare time, but nothing was accepted for production. Possibly, I was ahead of my time; what is acceptable today was less so in the early seventies.

Several years later, I attended a cluster of Christian colleges, to train for missionary work, where a Norwegian Lutheran minister arrived for a short break, funded by his mother. We played tennis and squash, attended lectures and became friends. He was an odd guy; quite serious and focused, but they say that opposites attract...

One day, he said that being in the pulpit is like being an actor, performing on stage. I have thought about this over the years, and perhaps there is some truth in his words. Certainly, successful preachers can attract and hold their audience - get their message across and help it stick. Personally, I always start a sermon with a joke, and I try to make dry liturgies interesting. Maybe my yearning to act has been a help, over the decades – you would need to ask my congregations.

Across the road from my digs in York, I met a lady in her thirties, who had written a book about her experiences with down-and-outs, in London. I often sat in her lounge, with her much older husband and his children, listening to her exploits with great interest. Tramps she had helped came to stay with her - one taught me how to make stew, from leftovers. Jem was a very intelligent and interesting man, and I gave him my granddad's suit, which I was keeping in reserve, as a thank-you.

Sally had become quite famous in certain circles, and one afternoon (my birthday, though that was a coincidence) Marianne Faithfull turned up, with an Irish aristocrat she was dating. She sat in a big armchair, talking, and put her wide-brimmed hat on the back of it. I just listened, nervous about joining the conversation, in such important company. When she left, she forgot her hat – I've no idea what happened to it, but I know I didn't dance off wearing it.

CHAPTER THREE

The In-Between Years…

The Start of Something

My youthful joy, at having finally arrived at what I considered to be the start of a successful and lucrative career, soon faded.

I remember well the advertising sales manager of the large newspaper group I worked for being utterly confused, when I announced that I was leaving to join N.C.H. Harrogate, as a housefather, for half of my current salary. But, it had seemed appropriate to apply to the children's housing charity.

At the age of fifteen, I had moved from my Church of England roots, where I was baptized and confirmed, to the Methodist Church. This was via a brief time spent with the then Congregational Church, now the United Reformed Church. Being caught in the toilets, at one of their Friday evening youth-club sessions, with a bottle of pale ale in each hand, my thumbs over the tops of the opened bottles, may have had something to do with my quick departure.

I was to remain with the Methodist Church for some twenty-five years, becoming a qualified local preacher and later working for the Norwegian Methodist Church, in Norway and Argentina - more of that later.

The N.C.H. home at Harrogate was a sprawling complex, with ten houses and a chapel, surrounding a large playing field. There were ten children in each house, all of which were run by an unmarried Methodist sister, or a married couple - the whole enterprise headed by a superintendent, his deputy and a matron. It has all been demolished now; home to a housing development.

This was my first introduction to the care system, of which I would become very knowledgeable, as the decades progressed. My stay at the children's home was informative, and often humorous.

The children attended local schools, and on Sunday mornings were marched, two-by-two, to the local Methodist church. One house, led by a Methodist sister, received particularly special treatment: on returning from Sunday church, after lunch, they always had to listen to Christian music, until teatime.

The superintendent was a Scottish local Methodist preacher, who ran a tight ship. My most unfortunate run-in with him was when I sought to produce a modern-day Nativity play, with young teenagers. The production did not last as long as I had hoped – in fact, it was all over in about twenty minutes. The local Methodist minister and his family arrived late, and we were already closing. It was embarrassing, to say the least, but it taught me a lot about working with teenage kids in the care system: mainly, their short attention span and competition for attention; the rehearsals had been a nightmare. But, nothing compared to being called to the superintendent's office, the next day, to explain how a children's Nativity play could be adapted to include young people going by bus to Bethlehem (and other artistic licence I had applied to the script). I had to do some quick thinking to get out of that one.

A married farming couple ran another house. The farmer was into tractors, and he became very upset when I allegedly left the tractor ignition on overnight, flattening the battery. The tractor was needed to mow the large playing field, and I had happily volunteered to undertake this duty, as I had never driven one before. Nor since.

And, not forgetting the little guy with a limp, who ran another house with his ample wife - a Yorkshire couple. He delighted in going about, cocking his leg at a settee and shouting "Peer Gynt Suite" (*"pee agint suite"*). He was called to the superintendent's notice one day, when he whipped round money from staff, for a bet on the upcoming Grand National. Gambling on Methodist premises was very much frowned upon.

One young man, keen on sport, claimed that he had only been turned down by a major football team because he had suffered from scarlet fever, as a child. He was fast on the football pitch – and, I suspected, in other ways, with his winning charm and boyish smile. He was also good with the children. His wife ran the house and he kept out of the way, as much as possible. This couple became firm friends with the farming couple.

There was great rivalry between the staff; the Methodist sisters kept themselves to themselves, and the married couples formed allegiances and dislikes. Just before my departure from N.C.H., the deputy superintendent - a Methodist minister - accused me of helping to break up a budding relationship, between a sister and a young, single deputy-housefather. At that time, I had worked in her house. I had befriended the young man, and admit I was a little confused by his relationship with this older woman. Still, it was none of my business, so when she asked me to post a letter to her family, saying that she thought the relationship was over, I obliged. The minister told me in no uncertain terms that I should not have posted the letter. It was at this point that the words "damned if you do and damned if you don't" first became clear to me.

One day, I talked with the deputy superintendent about training for probation work; I had decided that I wanted to be a probation officer. He advised me to take a pocketful of coins and ring around the universities which were offering such courses. I did so, and was offered an interview at Manchester University.

I was interviewed by a lady who remained silent throughout. I remember tapping my fingers lightly on the arm of my chair after ten minutes, and her staring at them in interest. Later, I realized that silence can be threatening, and is sometimes used to draw out people's emotions. Not *golden*, then? I wasn't offered a place on the course.

I was, however, accepted on a social-work course, at Liverpool University, which was sponsored by the Home Office. It was a two-year course, running from January 1972 to December 1973.

It was during this course that I also studied to become a Methodist local preacher and qualified, so when I would later move to West Sussex as a probation officer, I often conducted services in the local Methodist church on Sundays.

At Liverpool University, there was a vicar who taught Ethics, once a week. He told me: "If the bishop calls you in for a bollocking, the first thing to say, as you walk into the room, is 'Bishop, let us pray' - this always calms them down." I remembered that advice on several future occasions, though I would like to inform the vicar that his advice was not 100% accurate!

CHAPTER FOUR

The In-Between Years...

Probation Officer and Norway

Upon completing my social work studies at Liverpool University, I was offered a job as a probation officer, in a new town in West Sussex, built around a quaint, established residential area. The problems were immense: drugs, unemployment, lack of facilities for young people... times never seem to change.

I walked into my office on Monday morning, and found a huge stack of cases on the desk. I immediately panicked: how was I going to cope? The senior was off sick, so no help there.

I remember, at the time, interviewing clients by candlelight, as the miners were on strike. And, not being experienced in record keeping, I waffled endlessly into a Dictaphone, after each office and home visit, producing page after page of useless information. If only I had realized that the only requirement was "so and so reported; nothing new". When the chief probation officer came to do my confirmation visit, after my first year, he almost had a fit when I produced my records. What a waste of paper, he said, and my secretary's time.

On one occasion, I had to do a social enquiry report on a tubby, middle-aged man charged with shoplifting, to give the magistrates necessary background information. He was a rather sad man, and when I asked why he had been shoplifting, he looked me straight in the eye and replied: "So my wife would have sex with me!" This frustrated guy stole so he could give his wife presents, food or whatever, just to get into her good books. I can't remember what I wrote in the report, or how the court responded, but my recommendation was a probation order, with me as his probation officer, which he duly received.

I was once asked to sit in on an interview a direct entrant was to conduct, with a man charged with stealing women's underwear from washing lines. This middle-aged lady had just entered the probation service and was learning the ropes. She sat behind the desk in her office, the offender in front and me sitting at the back, thank goodness. When the man admitted to removing underwear and replacing it with a ten-bob notes, she asked the question I had been dreading: "Why do you do this?"

To which he replied: "To wear, of course!"

I nearly fell off my chair, trying not to laugh. Fortunately, I was staring at his back.

I contracted glandular fever in this job, which I am convinced I caught at a house where they kept coal in the bath, and in which my feet stuck to the filthy carpet. That's when I decided it was time to move on.

I was attracted to an advertisement in the *Daily Mail* for police inspectors in Hong Kong. *Yep, that's far enough away!* Instead, I actually went to Norway, to run a home for boys, aged twelve to eighteen, which was owned by the Norwegian Methodist Church.

I arrived in Norway in December 1974. It was very cold, with much snow, but amazing blue skies and sunshine.

First, I had to learn Norwegian.

I wanted to learn the language whilst earning a living, so I got a job as a helper, delivering beer and soft drinks, to restaurants in Oslo. Standing on the back of a lorry, wearing my granddad's long-johns, in minus-thirty degrees centigrade, and carrying full crates up six floors and empties down again, was a sobering experience. Additionally, getting up at dawn and trying to start an old Renault 4, with a six-volt battery, was challenging. Usually, it refused to start in the extreme cold, so I parked it on a slope at night, covering the engine with a blanket, and bumped it, as it gained speed on the steep hill. I rented an old, wooden house in a farmer's field, so no traffic problems doing this. Fortunately, too, the farmer was always up at the crack of dawn, with his snowplough.

After work, I attended Norwegian classes at a local school, and soon got the basics of the language. The lorry drivers I assisted were impressed - not with my lifting skills, but by my developing Norwegian. They spoke English to me at the beginning, but soon we switched to speaking Norwegian in the cab. When understanding each other was a problem, we would use a mixture of their reasonable English, my bad Norwegian and sign language.

After a couple of months, I was given my own route, and happily did deliveries on my own. I was always back at the depot long after the other drivers had gone home. One of the many reasons for my tardiness was often taking a bend too quickly, when the crates containing empty bottles had not been properly secured; I bet my broken bottles still remain in the hedge of some Norwegian church.

With a reasonable working knowledge of Norwegian, I went from driving the lorry to working in the boys' home.

The boys in the home could be difficult and required careful handing. Rejected by their families, for various reasons, some were petty criminals. Many nights I found myself sitting on the flat roof, smoking cigarettes, whilst waiting for one recalcitrant to return from a night of burglary. Then, being an appropriate adult at the local police station, later in the morning.

Whilst working there, I received a letter from a young couple in the

U.K., whose probation officer I had been in West Sussex. What a letter! Thanking me for understanding and helping them; for being a person they could talk to, and who listened. I think I still have it somewhere.

When I left the home, the boys presented me with a wooden cross, which they had made in our workshop, each signing the reverse with their name, in a black, felt-tip pen. It now hangs on the wall in my study, bringing back happy memories of us all fishing on a fjord, until the early hours, and singing "Bridge Over Troubled Waters" together, at a local Methodist Church - the boys always came with me when I conducted a church service. Later, I heard that one of them was killed in a crash, after stealing a car, leaving a baby daughter; another became a Pentecostal pastor. I often wonder what became of the others.

CHAPTER FIVE
Argentina

I left the boys' home to become a missionary, with an Indian tribe in Argentina - sent there by the Norwegian Methodist Church. Now I had another language to learn!

To be fair, the Methodist Bishop of Argentina spoke very good English, though I am not too sure he liked missionaries; he smiled benevolently and was pleasant enough, but there was always something hanging in the air when we met.

After I had flown to Buenos Aires, I went to the port to collect a couple of oil barrels, containing my belongings, which had been sent by sea, and found they had been broken into and robbed, the padlocks unceremoniously hacked off. This may have been because I had a British passport.

I was introduced to a German Methodist missionary by the bishop. I found the minister very welcoming, and we talked for a long time about the importance of social work in any church ministry. I went to the children's home he ran with his wife and was impressed; they had founded it with funds from their German church. I wish I'd had the opportunity to work with this couple, but the bishop had other plans for me.

I initially stayed at the faculty for training Christian ordinands from several denominations, in Buenos Aires. It was rather basic, and my mattress was ancient, with a huge lump in the middle. When I enquired if there was another room available, the supervisor showed me one with a large hole in the roof, the expression on his face saying: *Try this one, you dissatisfied Englishman.* I met a lady called Rosa, who was the receptionist - a helpful and cheerful soul. She had an amazing knowledge of Buenos Aires and could point me in the right direction, to whatever I needed to know.

I once broke a tooth and needed a dentist, so Rosa gave me a name and address. I will never forget the dentist's name: Dr. Busafusco. He did not speak English so, after examining the tooth, we communicated by paper and pencil; he wrote down the price of a gold crown and a stainless-steel one. I looked at all the zeros after the figures, and quickly wrote "Si" after the stainless-steel option. Still, it has lasted for forty years, so not a bad choice.

Buenos Aires was often subjected to unexpected power cuts, all over the city. I had just arrived for one appointment, when everything went black; I didn't need the doc to explain that I would have to come back another day. I became used to the power cuts; they were part and parcel of daily life at the time.

At the offices of the Methodist church in Buenos Aires, I was introduced to those who ran the church with the bishop. They included the accountant: an awkward man, of Italian background. He clearly did not like missionaries and showed this at every opportunity. It was a cleft stick: the church needed the support of Methodists from around the world, but seemed to prefer hard cash, rather than being sent workers.

Inflation was running at one-thousand percent, and it was difficult to understand my monthly stipend from Norway, as converted to Argentine pesos. The accountant used a strange rate of exchange, which seemed to favour the church, rather than me. I quickly learnt to use banks to exchange money, as they always offered favourable rates of exchange, which changed daily. The main exchange currency was American dollars, and rates advertised outside the banks used this as their main currency of exchange. One dollar could be exchanged into thousands of Argentine pesos; another lesson for me: the rich get richer and the poor get poorer. I reflected on this, as I passed numerous ladies sitting on the streets, selling a few oranges or lemons for coppers, to feed their children, whilst those fortunate enough to own a house saw their investment rocketing. Those who had the cash to buy a car did so immediately, as a delay of one month would see prices double.

Whilst attending Spanish classes in Buenos Aires, I took services in English, at a Methodist church on the outskirts on Sunday mornings, and at an ecumenical church in the evenings. The church on the outskirts was a mainly North American congregation: people from big corporations, who were working in Buenos Aires, and from the American Embassy. As I stood on the platform, conducting services, I could periodically see the tops of machine guns pass the window, as security guards for the better-off members of the congregation patrolled outside. The thought of a master in the congregation giving the shoot signal crossed my mind a few times, as I delivered my sermon.

The other church was a much poorer congregation, mainly descended from British families who had moved to Argentina for various reasons, including religious persecution. There was quite a contrast on a Sunday: rich people in the morning, and the poor in the evening.

Eddie was a member of the latter congregation. His parents had moved to Argentina from the U.K. and he himself had never visited the U.K. But, in language and thinking he was clearly British, his attitudes reflecting the British lower-middle class. Eddie seemed to dislike Argentinian life, even though he had been raised and educated in that system; he was a Brit, through and through. The Falklands War was on the horizon, and I was back in Norway when it broke out, wondering how people like Eddie were surviving.

An incident on a train, a few weeks after my arrival, confirmed my thoughts about the fraught Anglo/Argentine situation. A man in the seat opposite saw my British passport and started shouting: "Las Malvinas son Argentinos!!" – *"The Falklands are Argentine!!"* It reminded me of a Glaswegian who had once stood opposite me, on an overcrowded train, from London to Glasgow, drunk and wanting a fight. As we stood all the way, in a confined space, at the end of the carriage, he periodically menaced me with the question: "D'yer wanna fight, Jimmy?"

There were members of the poorer congregation with proud Welsh roots. Though they had never visited Wales, they kept the language and traditions; their meagre homes were adorned with the Welsh flag, beautiful pictures and handmade objects. It is said that Buenos Aires is a melting pot for many cultural backgrounds; I quickly became aware of this.

During my time with the rich congregation I enjoyed the hospitality of several families. The military attaché to the American embassy found my wearing Norwegian clogs at services fascinating, and he took a shine to me. On one occasion, the American ambassador attended a church service I was conducting - he was not impressed, as I inadvertently stood in his place of honour, whilst he and the other dignitaries stood in line outside. Oh well, the clogs still had it.

An American couple had established a Bible study group in their apartment. He was a journalist and correspondent for an American newspaper; his wife a musician and piano teacher. They had a young son and daughter, who were spoilt, and took mischievous delight in getting other children into trouble, by blaming them for their own misdoings; they were always believed. The journalist was a big man with a beard – a loudmouth, know-it-all personality; his small, quieter wife was more inclined to listen to reason. Their weekly Bible studies should have been entitled "The Interpretation According to Joe", and were frequently interrupted by bad behaviour from their kids, who ratted to their maid that the other kids had misbehaved, knowing that the maid would tell Dad. And, that Dad would defend them to the hilt.

The Church Council met for lunch every Friday, at the American embassy, and I was invited, by virtue of my status as their interim minister. Steaks the size of the plate were the order of the day, with a heap of chips. Unfortunately for me, I had decided before leaving Norway that Fridays would be my fast day. The yanks were not impressed, as they dug into their steaks, whilst I humbly sipped a glass of water. Their glares spoke volumes: *why is this weird Brit here; he belongs in the pulpit, with his clogs.* To be fair I did have support and tolerance from most of the guys and gals.

My main adversary was the chair of the council: an Anglo-Argentine, who had been high up in a global accounting company. He appeared to consider me a disappointment: a lay minister who wore inappropriate footwear, when conducting services.

Church councils love to discuss money, or rather the lack of. Talk of replacing stained-glass windows or stolen lead on the roof was fine; talk about mission and spreading the Gospel, and the shutters come down - on the incumbent's fingers. And, why should these high-flying guys and gals be any different? They were a cross-section of many church councils, in any part of the world; they were only comfortable discussing things they understood.

The bishop's plan was for me to go south, to a town called Neuquen, and get involved with the Methodist church there, which needed help in their desire to work with the Mapuche Indians, nearby. I learnt that there were Mapuche Indian tribes in southern Argentina and southern Chile, who crossed the border frequently, to the suspicion of both governments.

So, the time approached for me to start the work the Argentine Methodist Church had invited me over for, and I moved from Buenos Aires to the south of Argentina.

I was due to fly down to meet the Methodist minister of the church in Neuquen - the town nearest to the land where the Mapuche Indians lived, though still an hour's drive away.

The day before my visit, I lay sunbathing in the garden of the house owned by the Buenos Aires congregation (the rich one), which was a big mistake, as the sun was fierce and the following morning my back was so burnt I couldn't sit down. On the 'plane I sat leaning forward, for the entire hour-long flight, and when I arrived at the minister's home I was in agony.

He was born in Chile, his wife Argentinian. He didn't speak English, though his wife and father-in-law who lived nearby did. After an evening together, I slept gingerly, and the following morning he drove me to Piedra del Aguila (*Stone of the Eagle*), where I was to live. He showed me a small, dilapidated shack, which had been accommodation for local workers. It was empty, apart from fragmented beef carcasses literally hanging around the place - even in the shower – even though nobody had lived there for quite some while. And, plenty of rubbish, too. Fortunately, it turned out that this hovel was not to be my residence, as the congregation rented a small house in Neuquen.

From there, we drove a short distance to part of the Pampas, left the road and went on a dirt track for some while, before arriving at a settlement of makeshift shacks, with Mapuches sitting around outside, and sheep in pens. I began to understand that my vision of North American Indians was way off target: these were gauchos, who eked out a living from grazing and eating sheep. And, drinking as much alcohol as they could get! That was to be my work: encouraging them to be less alcohol-dependent. The minister told me that the Roman Catholic Church had agreed to welfare work with the tribe, but no missionary work: that was *their* territory.

After introductions, we sat in a circle and drank *mate*, a traditional South American, caffeine-rich drink. It is prepared by steeping dried leaves of yerba mate in hot water, in a hollow calabash gourd, and drunk collectively, through a bombilla, or straw. For the poor, this straw is made of hollow-stemmed cane; for the richer, stainless steel; and, silver for the well off. I studied the red cheeks of the tribal elders, as I watched the brew being passed around the group; was I likely to catch T.B., I wondered. When my turn came, I sucked slowly out of the cane bombilla - not bad. I passed it on, with a polite smile and a prayer.

On a later visit, I was allowed to view from a distance, as the Mapuches conducted a sacred ceremony, in honour of those who had been killed when the Argentine government tamed Patagonia's wilderness and made Argentina a modern nation, under Julio Argentino Roca - an army general who served as president, from 1880-86, and 1898-1904. His barbaric "conquest of the desert" campaign, in the late 1870s, saw some thousand Indians slaughtered, their land shared out amongst cronies.

The Falklands War was looming, and Brits were viewed with much suspicion.

One day, in Buenos Aires, I was on a collectivo (a small bus, on which passengers hang from all over the vehicle), when I saw a soldier staring at me. I realized that I must have looked suspicious to him, with my beard and my ex-Army Stores khaki cotton hat pulled down; the embodiment of Che Guevara. The soldier continued to stare, until I alighted. Then, he followed me. I groaned: *What now?* After a couple of blocks, though, he lost me – or, rather, I lost him... with a lesson learnt.

In populated areas everywhere were military with machine guns - virtually every street corner in Buenos Aires. *Keep on walking; don't hesitate; don't stare and don't look back* - Andrew's homespun survival code.

I once discovered that driving a friend's car down a one-way street was not a good idea. I had no idea that it was one-way traffic, until suddenly this old guy jumped in the car and told me to drive to the police station. When I did, he took me inside and I was told to sit down, whilst other guys in civvies gathered round, staring at me and mumbling to each other. We clearly had a communication problem, and upon examining my British passport, their expressions became fierce.

Later, I understood that the poorly paid police officers were not averse to accepting a cash bribe for traffic offences. I must have instinctively fished a few peso notes from my pocket, and was thankfully shown the door.

On another occasion, I was pulled up for allegedly speeding in Patagonia, in an old Willis American jeep. One doesn't argue the toss, so when a uniformed officer jumped out of his car menacingly, holding up his hand, I paid the "fine" without question.

Oh yes, the jeep? Well, I needed transport when I arrived in Neuquen, so I bought a second world war Willis jeep, cheap. *Jeepers creepers!* It went okay, but one day, when crossing Patagonia, in the heat of the day, it suddenly stopped. On examination, I found that the carburettor was leaking petrol and the tank was empty - miles from anywhere, with vast wilderness on all sides, and no sign of any vehicle! I looked up and down the long, straight road; what a Godforsaken place to die. *No way, Jose.*

I had the foresight to carry a full jerry can, and bits of cloth, which I tied around the carburettor. I poured the fuel into the tank and the engine fired. The only problem now was would I find a petrol station, before the few litres ran out?

No chance! After thirty kilometres, she conked out again, and it was back to square one. I waited in the back of the jeep, in as much shade as I could muster. And, waited. And, waited. I hadn't seen another vehicle all day. I guess I eventually prayed.

Then, half an hour later, a car appeared, on the glittering horizon! The next vehicle could be hours away, and it would soon be dark, so I stood in the middle of the road, waving my arms and pointing to the jeep, leaving the driver no choice but to stop, or run me down. The angel stopped. Taking tow-rope from his boot, he hitched up the jeep and indicated for me to get into the car.

We drove in silence, for about an hour, and he pulled into a garage, in a small community of just a few houses. He unhitched the jeep, and with a smile and a wave, he was gone.

I managed to make the mechanic understand the problem, and in just a few minutes with his tools, it was fixed. I filled the tank, with the few pesos I had in my pocket, but the mechanic wouldn't take any recompense for his time and trouble, God bless him. Then I was off, back to some sort of civilization.

Explain that one.

The Methodist church in Neuquen was obviously not poor - the working folk either professionals or tradesmen – and, as mentioned, they had rented a small bungalow for me. Not a palace, by any stretch of the imagination, but liveable, and a massive improvement on the dilapidated workers' shack. Boy, was I pleased to see it that day?

I sat in the tiny lounge and pondered how I could help the Mapuches. Cheap alcohol seemed a necessity to survive their tough, daily existence. I reflected on how Christians want to do good – most, anyway.

Then, it hit me: the Methodist bishop had been offered a social worker by the Norwegian Methodist Church as a "missionary"; there must have been contact between him and the minister in Neuquen, and it became known that I was on offer. The reality was that the good folk in Neuquen, who wanted to help the Mapuches (at the instigation of their minister, I suspect), had not fully thought through the practicalities. So, now they had an Englishman from Norway, with little Spanish, trying to help Indians who probably didn't want it.

I further reflected on this, as I wandered around a local supermarket, suddenly feeling very lonely. Then, when ABBA's "Dancing Queen" blasted out through the speakers, I felt more at home.

Early one afternoon, I rang the doorbell of a flat owned by a member of the congregation, and the architect came to the door in his pyjamas, rubbing his eyes and yawning. *Funny,* I thought. That was my first understanding of siesta time, and he wasn't best pleased. I can't remember why I wanted to see him, but I will never forget his expression.

I consider that preaching in other languages than one's own focuses the mind on what one wants to say; no wittering on with limited vocabulary. One Sunday morning, I was asked by the minister to deliver the sermon to his Neuquen congregation.

Verses from John's Gospel though the exact text escapes me now, and it certainly escaped the congregation then. As I stood at the front and attempted to expound the text, in my very limited Spanish, I looked around, as they politely smiled and nodded. And, I thought: *You don't understand a blooming word, do you?* Roll on the gift of tongues.

I have sometimes been apprehensive that God might call me to serve in China, and how I would cope with learning Mandarin. Useful when ordering in a Chinese restaurant, though; would certainly impress the waiter, although he would undoubtedly speak good English.

There were a couple of guys in the Neuquen congregation, whom I will never forget. They owned a plumbing business, and latched onto me like glue. One was called Cacho - a lovely man of Italian heritage, who taught me how to test if spaghetti is cooked, by throwing some at the kitchen tiles: if it sticks, it is done. I spent happy hours with Cacho, his wife Alicia and their family; a comfort in all the chaos. His partner, Carlos, had hoped to be a Methodist minister. They had a proposition for me.

Before I write another word, my explanation for my actions is based on loneliness, the desire to please my new friends and to be a success with my mission.

They knew I had some American dollars in a bank account, provided by the Norwegian Methodist Church, for a rainy day. Their proposition went like this: they needed to buy supplies for their plumbing business and, with inflation running at a thousand percent, prices were rising every day. So, they wanted me to fly with them to Buenos Aires, lend them some money from the account so they could buy materials and, after a couple of months, when they had received the money from their work, they would repay me, and pay for my return flight, as the bank was in Buenos Aires.

I didn't like it. Firstly, it was not my money, and secondly, I didn't know if I could trust them. What if they refused to pay the money back? But, if I refused, they could scupper my work with the Mapuches, by actively working against me; telling their minister they didn't want me there - who would tell the bishop, who would then tell the Norwegians... I decided to help myself, by helping them.

The three of us flew to the capital and I loaned them the money. Whilst they were buying materials and arranging transport, I went to a cinema and watched the new movie *Kramer vs. Kramer*, with English subtitles, and that night we flew back to Neuquen.

They repaid the loan, as agreed, and I repaid the money into the bank account, with a huge sigh of relief. No harm done, then…

The reality of the mission work did not turn out as the congregation had envisaged. It became clear to them what I had once learnt as a training officer: the six Ps: "Poor Planning Produces Piss Poor Performance."

As I was packing my meagre belongings, for my return to Norway, another strange thing happened.

I had advertised for locals to come to my house at a certain time, if they wanted to buy anything; I was showing bits and pieces in the lounge, such as a camera and portable stereo. I realized there was a guy missing. When the eager, inflation-conscious buyers departed, I went into the bedroom, where my jacket was hanging, behind the door. Being a creature of habit, I had left my wallet in the inside pocket – I now found that it was gone.

The strange part is that, against all my instincts, I had removed my Argentine identity document, which was now safely in my trouser pocket. Without that, I would have had great difficulty leaving the country and boarding my flight, booked for a couple of days later.

CHAPTER SIX

Back to Norway

After returning to Norway from Argentina, I decided more driving therapy was needed - not beer lorries, but buses.

I needed to take an H.G.V. bus test, so I enrolled with a local driving centre. The tutor took me out in a Scania bus - a coach, as they don't have double-decker buses in Norway. It was great fun, driving around the town and fjord. I only had cash for three lessons, but in my humble opinion that was sufficient.

So, to the test. First, I had to pass a written exam: a mathematical calculation, of how many tonnes of weight are allowed on certain roads. This was for the lorry part of the test, as they did not give separate licences for H.G.V. and buses; it was a combined driving licence. Hey ho, I passed the written test first time. Then came the driving test. The private bus company I intended working for lent me a bus, and off we went, from the test centre - myself and the examiner.

It was a spring day, with no snow. All was going well, until we passed a lady, walking on the pavement towards the bus. I was driving a left-hand drive bus, of course, with the gearstick on my right; passengers boarded on the right-hand side, at the front of the bus, and alighted at the rear, on the same side. I clearly saw the lady approaching, but there was a lot of water at the side of the road, after the snow had melted. *Splash!*

"Stop!" shouted the examiner.

I pulled up, as quickly as possible, and in the right-hand wing mirror, to my horror, I saw the lady, absolutely drenched. The examiner told me to open the front door, and he got out to apologize to the poor lady. I also got out and apologized, under his withering glare. I asked if I could pay to dry-clean her coat, but she declined. As she walked away, and the examiner and I returned to the bus, I thought to myself: *Failed this one.*

Afterward, he remonstrated with me about watching for such hazards. And, yep, I failed.

The manager of the bus company was not impressed when I had to take the test again, but this time I passed. So, after going with experienced drivers to learn all the routes, I started my bus driving career in earnest.

The town routes were fairly easy and the fares were fixed, so I had no problem with the ticket machine, perched next to me. Driving on the fjord routes was much more exciting, though, with narrow roads and sharp bends, but varying ticket prices.

My shifts started at 4 a.m. or 1 p.m. In the winter, for the early morning shift, I would trudge through the snow to the bus station, my beard and nostril hair frozen, as I carried my company bag, containing my ticket machine and a large flask of hot tomato soup. The buses were parked by the bus station. The first job was to disconnect the oil warmer and crack up. Then, after making sure the interior heaters were working, I would drive off around the fjord to collect passengers, bringing them into town to catch their trains, to start work in Oslo at 8 a.m.

On my maiden trip, I missed the first pick-up point, by the fjord, flying past a lady in her dressing gown, who was accompanying a school youth. I managed to find the other passengers, and my empty bus gradually filled, until it was packed with people, standing the length of the gangway. When I got back to the bus station, the manager was not happy: the lady had angrily rung him, having had to send her son to college in a taxi, which the bus company now had to pay for. I never made that mistake again.

On the maiden trip I reversed, slightly, into another bus. The streets in the town were narrow, and one came to a T-junction, with railings ahead; it required nifty manoeuvring to make the necessary right turn. Thinking I wouldn't make the turn, I reversed a little, not noticing the bus behind me, almost on my rear bumper. The driver gesticulated from his seat as I reversed into his grille, a signal I duly noted in my wing mirror. He subsequently complained to the rival bus company - mine.

And, ticket prices…

There was no problem with the regulars, going to work in town, or to catch a train, as they had monthly passes; all I had to do was check, as they streamed past, that the pass was up to date. The problem arose when I collected crowds in town, on the afternoon shift: they were all paying cash and going to different destinations. I would park in the bus lay-by, and on they flooded. If I understood where they were going, I simply punched the ticket price into the machine, and out came their ticket; the problems arose if I didn't understand where they were going. It was embarrassing to keep asking, then look through my table of rates. So, on these occasions, I developed my own system: charge the lowest amount - this resulted in several very happy passengers.

I became adept at driving buses of various models. The best, in my opinion, was the Scania, known as "King of the Road" vehicles - five manual forward gears and a clutch. In town, Volvos were used, with automatic gearboxes for the steep hills. My own downfall was the DAF semi-automatic: a gear lever, but no clutch, with a motor brake on the floor, to the left of the brake pedal, which was used to slow the engine.

I was going down a hill in winter, with the DAF half full, and decided that I needed to slow the vehicle down. Using the foot brake is not advisable in snowy conditions, so I applied the motor brake, with my left foot. I held my foot on the motor brake for too long, the engine stalled and the bus careered under a low bridge, landing in a snow drift, at the side of the road - shaken passengers and a shaky driver.

There is a saying in Norwegian which roughly translates: *"A bus chauffeur, a bus chauffeur; he is a man of good humour,"* - the translation misses the rhyming Norwegian poetry. I did try to be a chauffeur of good humour, but admittedly there were occasional lapses, like when passengers got on and produced a high-value Norwegian kroner banknote, for a short journey; I have been known to hunch my shoulders angrily, and announce into the large, interior mirror, to anyone interested: "What do they think I am? A bloomin' bank?" In Norwegian, of course.

I enjoyed driving around the fjord of an evening, looking at the water lapping the shoreline, as the sun was setting. I would drive out with an empty bus, for about forty minutes, and was to wait until the appointed timetable departure time, before driving back to town. There were hardly any passengers on the return journey. One evening, my rebellious streak took control: I waited way over my appointed departure time, then drove like a racing driver, around the narrow roads.

Two problems.

The first was when I almost hit a bus from the same company, on a vicious bend. On his return, the driver reported to the duty inspector that he had met Rea (they pronounced it *Ree-ar*) by the fjord, driving like a pig! *Me? Never, Herr Inspector! Pure exaggeration, sir; pure exaggeration.*

By this juncture, I had had three minor mishaps reported, with other buses in town, so the law of probability was not on my side. But, boy, could I handle a bus on narrow, bendy roads? It was going to my head. I think it was the same mad evening - when I allegedly drove like a pig - that I picked up a passenger, along the fjord, on my return journey. The bus was empty when he climbed aboard, and he sat on the front seat - on the right-hand side, of course. I gave him his ticket, slipped his coins into the bag, slung beneath the ticket machine, then into first gear and off with the handbrake. And then, I forgot all about him!

He returned to my consciousness when, after negotiating a difficult bend at speed, I glanced over and saw that he had pulled his raincoat over his head, probably in terror. Oh well; yer pays yer money and yer takes yer chances. To my knowledge, no report to management. A lucky escape, and for him.

Two other bus incidents spring to mind.

The first was when I was doing a daily run, driving a group of teenage college students and teachers home from town, and dropping them off at various points in the country. After several alighted at the first drop-off point, I engaged first gear (Scania manual gearbox), and... nothing. I let the clutch out fully, whilst still in gear, but the engine just revved...

I used the radio to converse with an inspector – or, rather, *attempted* to converse. By this time, my Norwegian was fairly fluent, but this was a time of stress: the youngsters and their teachers just wanted to get home. I rattled on about the inspector needing to send a replacement bus, as my clutch had gone. After my first wave of frustrated words, a message came back to repeat the whole thing again. I did, and eventually another bus arrived. The grumbling passengers changed buses; I waited for a tow truck.

The second notable incident was when I was driving in winter, and stopped to pick up two elderly ladies. Fares paid, they seated themselves, and... the air brakes wouldn't release.

As the two ladies shouted despairingly from the centre of the bus that they had a train to catch, I radioed the duty inspector.

"Oh yes, Ree-ar; the air brakes have frozen. Have you got any timetables aboard?"

Thinking it was a ridiculous reply, I looked around and saw a few timetables; I replied that there were.

"Okay, have you got a lighter?"

I desperately needed a smoke, but having once been caught smoking my pipe by the company manager, as he passed me in his car (I was driving an empty bus at the time), I wasn't going to get caught again. And, it was too damn cold to smoke outside.

Receiving my reply that I did have a lighter in my pocket, the inspector replied: "Okay, crawl under the bus and try to free the air brakes using lighted timetables." Inspectors know best; that's what they're paid for.

I got out of the bus, with some timetables and my lighter. Watched through the windows with suspicion, by the few passengers, I slid underneath the bus, assisted by the ice, where I lit some timetables, held the flame against the air brake junction and prayed that the whole bus wouldn't explode in flames. No mi culpa this time if it did; only following orders.

Then, I got back in the bus and... Hey ho: the air brakes released themselves. Off we jolly well went - a happy, confused driver and even happier passengers.

My final act with the bus company was to wash my car in their car park, with their equipment, in winter. Just outside the bus workshop there was a spray machine, for washing the buses. My shift had ended on that Saturday afternoon, so I was on my own time. The machine made an excellent job of cleaning my car. The only downside was that I was wearing a pair of tanned leather cowboy boots, of which I was very proud; they went well with my medium blue uniform. But, slippery leather soles and ice, unfortunately, do not perform well together.

The duty inspector had been observing me, through his office window. He was a pleasant and sympathetic man, who seemed to take this rogue Englishman under his wing. He opened the window and suggested that I drive my car into the bus garage to dry. *Nice thought.* So, I slid open the huge doors and drove my car in, parking it over a service pit.

As I walked around the pit, to the doors, I must have slipped on some oil, and went crashing into the bottom of the pit, where I landed on my back. I lay there, in agony, for some time, eventually thinking that I had to get out, or I might be there until Monday morning. Gingerly, I rolled onto my stomach, raised myself slowly and staggered to the steps. I got out of the pit, where I managed to get into my car and reverse it out.

Although there was a huge lump at the base of my spine, which prevented me sitting comfortably in the driver's seat, I drove slowly to the hospital, not far away and, after parking, I reported to Emergency. I was admitted and, grateful to be lying in a bed, waited until a junior doctor examined me. He sent me for an x-ray, and later came to inform me that I had broken my back.

The following day was Sunday. It was not a joyful day, as I lay there, imagining the consequences of the incident.

On Monday morning, what I assumed was a registrar came in, holding the x-ray: I had not broken my back; the junior doctor had seen an existing curvature of my spine and confused it with a break. I could go home. *Hallelujah!* I didn't tell him about the big, black dots I had seen, as I lay staring at the ceiling, for the whole previous day. Minor concussion, probably; it would pass… It did.

Whilst driving buses I attended Oslo University, to study theology.

I met many students who were doing a six-year degree course, intending to be ordained in the Lutheran Church of Norway. Their matter-of-fact attitude amazed me: they did not seem interested in discussing what they were taught, but simply accepting it. I wanted to challenge much of the teaching, but I kept my mouth shut. I did not intend upon being ordained, just to learn more about a subject which fascinated me.

Driving my ancient Peugeot estate car to the university one morning, I exceeded the speed limit on the dual carriageway - probably a mixture of tardiness, as usual, and reminiscing that I was driving my bus around the fjord.

Then, an unmarked police car pulled up alongside, and the passenger waved a paddle at me out of the window, to pull over. I got a fine.

A couple of days later, I was at the university, sitting in class. And, directly opposite me was the police officer with the paddle, who had issued the fine. I think he recognized me, too, but we didn't speak. I mentally forgave him, for it was my transgression. I wondered what he was doing, studying theology; he would have no doubt thought the same about me.

CHAPTER SEVEN

Going it Alone

I attended the local Methodist church and preached, now and again, in Norwegian.

During one service, I played the guitar and sang a song I had composed. I can only strum basic guitar chords, and my singing is abysmal. I saw the organist out of the corner of my eye, listening intently; his facial expression registered pain and disbelief. But, I'd had a go. Never again.

The Methodist minister was, in my experience, a creep. Upon arrival, he refused, point blank, to reside with his family in the flat next to the church, where previous ministers had lived. Fair enough, the congregation bought a most pleasant detached, wooden house in the town. Most houses in Norway are built from plentiful wood, and are designed to withstand the cold temperatures. He had this habit of twitching his nose, when he disapproved of something.

One day, he rang me to suggest that I would make a good arranger of services. I cannot remember the official title, but being an arranger is what the post amounted to; I would be on the church council. The voluntary post involved arranging preachers to take services - although the minister took the majority, there were times when he was not available. I said yes, later realizing that it was a role no one else wanted to undertake.

My main sin was to become friendly with a member of the congregation, greatly disapproved of by the minister, because the man opposed and criticized him at every opportunity. Every congregation has those who quietly - or loudly - do not like or agree with the leader's actions, and Svein (name changed to protect the guilty) was loud. An engineer by profession, with a "spade is a spade" outlook on life, I became friends with Svein because I liked his devil-may-care approach.

What I did not understand, until much later, was that he had an eye for young women. I don't think he ever followed through, but his eye undoubtedly roamed.

He was married to a Pentecostal lady, who was lovely, but strict, and who stayed in the congregation, even though she frowned at baby baptism and other non-Pentecostal practices. Their daughter was also a member of the congregation, with her husband, and did not talk to her father. Perhaps I should have delved more deeply into this rift, but at the time I put it down to her being loyal to her mother.

I persevered in the congregation, until I started a house church - this met on Wednesday and Sunday evenings, at my home. A varied group of people attended - mainly recovering alcoholics and drug addicts, although there was a police detective and his wife; an interesting combination. I became friendly with the detective and his wife, and found them very sincere and supportive of me and my endeavours. House fellowships are important: people can talk together, study Scripture and pray, in an informal way, outside the confines of church services.

A new minister came to the Methodist church, and when I mentioned his name people pulled a face, commenting that his track record was uninspiring, and he was boring. I had already decided to go my own way, prior to his arrival, and I went to see him, saying that I was leaving the congregation. His reaction was predictably matter-of-fact and boring: he said he would need to fill in a form.

One Wednesday evening, a big chap of about thirty-five was praising in tongues on my lounge floor. The following morning, I was called to collect him from a bench at the railway station, where he was drunk out of his mind. He came to most of my house meetings, and usually behaved himself; he knew his Bible.

It was also about this time that Svein's obsession with young women became apparent. He attended my meetings, as did a recovering drug addict, in her late twenties. Through her I gained an understanding of how recovering addicts, who become Christians, can go from nothing to off-the-scale, concerning Bible knowledge and prayer, speaking fluently in tongues. I noticed Svein staring at her, with a weird expression on his face, and being over-anxious to provide practical assistance. This is part and parcel of trying to help, but there has to be a line. I guess he felt lonely and found young people - especially women - inspiring. He was a lecturer at a local college.

One couple who came also stand out. They had attended a Baptist church in town, but the husband fell out with the pastor. Warning bells rang, so I took an opportunity to ring the pastor. I found out that, in his opinion, the husband was a troublemaker; ministers feel threatened by members of their congregation who oppose them and are not supportive. Congregations seem to fit into three groups: those who are supportive and understanding of their minister; those who attend services and remain quiet; those who oppose any changes and bring their own opinions and experiences to the table. It reminds me of a joke, about a new vicar arriving and saying to the churchwarden:

"How long have you been here?"

"Fifty years."

"Ah, you must have seen many changes."

"Yes, and I've opposed every one!"

It was at this point that I started to understand more of the problems of ministry, and it put me off any thought of full-time ministry.

Still, I tried to form a good relationship with this couple. One Sunday afternoon, we were walking in a forest, and I mentioned that I was thinking about doing a mission. The man suggested asking Cliff Richard to come over - not sure how that idea came up, but he seemed to think it a good one. That should have set alarm bells clanging in my head, but I persevered, until it became clear that he was criticizing me behind my back, and trying to pinch members of the house church, for something he had in mind. I can't remember how the situation panned out, but the couple eventually left.

One guy who came to the house church was a recovering alcoholic, called Willy. He had been sober for a long time and seemed to be doing well. He was a good Christian (whatever that means), knew his Bible and always prayed when we were together. Willy formed the notion that he was Moses and I was Aaron – apparently, there had been another Aaron before me, but he fell from grace… Willy's grace, anyway. I should have been more wary of this Moses/Aaron duo act, but at the time I was still somewhat naïve about these matters; Willy intrigued me with his faith and piety, and several of the house church would wander around uninhabited spots in summer, I suppose imagining that we were Jesus and His disciples. Anyway, we got this idea that God was calling us to open a centre for alcoholics and drug addicts. Willy had been there, done it, got the T-shirt, and pulled through; raw spirit ruins the internal organs - not least the brain.

Consumed with this idea that we had to open a Christian home for those in need, one afternoon we came across a farmer, ploughing his field. Willy and I looked at each other: this was it! I took my cue, left the group and strode purposely to the farmer, on his tractor. He reduced the throttle and stared at me, expectantly. I explained that God had called us to start a

Christian home for recovering alcoholics and drug addicts, and that he was to give us part of his land, and help us build it.

I still cringe, when I think of this episode of madness. And, I fervently hope that the farmer did not understand, because of my poor Norwegian or bad accent. He just sat and stared at me; maybe he thought we'd all escaped from a mental home. He eyed me, then the group, shrugged and gunned the throttle. That was the end of that, thank goodness. Of all the crazy ideas I have had, this one had to be in the top ten; probably top five...

For a short period, I worked in a halfway house in Oslo, run by the council, for men who were well on the way to sobriety and ready to move into their own accommodation. Some had lost their homes and families from their addiction to alcohol, and deserved a second chance.

In my few months at the halfway house I had joyful and sad experiences. Men moved on to successfully to rebuild their life; others were less fortunate. Some had been reduced to drinking car-window washer fluid.

The men had their own rooms with a T.V., and they liked to show off their proficiency in the English language to this Englishman. The average age of the residents was about fifty-plus; many had been sailors, with good English. Norwegians over a certain age hadn't learnt English at school, but followed the English-speaking programmes with subtitles (Norwegian television showed several American and British series); when I was running a weekly Bible study group at the Methodist church, the evenings *Dynasty* was on always resulted in a low attendance.

On one particular night there had been quite a few laughs, as one of the guys had been watching *Falcon Crest*, an American series. He had laughingly called the programme *Falcon Stress*, and we had joked about the unlikely plot. It had been a good evening, and soon they were settling down to sleep.

Folk who have slept rough for a long time do not follow normal routines. At about 2 a.m. on this night, one guy started cooking a fry-up, in the communal kitchen, and I had to point out the house rule about not cooking between certain hours. I was patiently attempting to explain (in Norwegian) why he could not fry eggs and bacon in the early hours, when another resident ran into the kitchen, exclaiming that Harald had gone out - a man in his thirties.

Staff worked alone at night, and I was not supposed to leave the building, but I felt I had no choice but to try to find Harald, if he was not too far away.

I found him, some two-hundred metres from the house, lying dead in a pile of snow, with an empty bottle of screen-washer fluid by his side. Thirty-five years later, the scene still haunts me.

I needed a permanent job, and one afternoon I got down on my knees in the lounge and prayed, earnestly: "Lord, I need work. Please."

Literally five minutes later the 'phone rang.

I had been working for a security firm, on an ad hoc basis, and enjoyed it - driving around all night in a Volkswagen Golf, checking factories on a fjord, nursing homes and other establishments in need of security checks. The voice at the end of the 'phone was one of the managers at the security firm, and he offered me a permanent job, working seventeen-hour shifts, three times a week.

I would start at IKEA in Oslo, from 4 p.m. to 11 p.m., then drive a couple of kilometres up the road, to what was then the main airport in Oslo, staying until 8 a.m., to guard the bonded warehouse. I would then return to IKEA for two hours, whilst staff checked in, before going home to bed.

The pay wasn't brilliant, but I had time to think in peace, and pray. At IKEA, I would walk around all the departments at regular intervals, all night, in my smart, blue security uniform, inserting keys - which were screwed to walls in strategic positions - into my machine. This was to record where I had inspected, and at what time, and the reason was twofold: firstly, so the security company could prove their employees were doing their job, and secondly, so companies had proof for their insurers, should an incident occur; a wonderful idea, like so many things. At the end of my shift, I left my machine at the security firm's offices, where an inspector removed the roll and replaced it with a new one, ready for my next shift. The truth that practice is not perfect was revealed to me one morning, when I was resting on a settee in the office, after a night shift, and an inspector arrived to open my machine. A roll of crumpled paper fell to the floor: useless. No recordings; only smudged ink. Oh, dear… Well, the principle was excellent.

One night, on duty at IKEA, I passed a whipped ice-cream machine on my round. It was a hot evening and it looked tempting; surely the company wouldn't begrudge me a free cornet? I had often seen customers buying cornets as they walked past the counter, the only difference being that they paid the market price. I removed a cornet from the pile, placed it under the nozzle and pulled the lever, expectantly.

I didn't get what I expected: cream-coloured, watery liquid shot out, all over my tailor-made uniform – and, I mean *all over*. I had no idea that when the store closed the staff would flush the machine through with water. I had to sit in it all night - until the next morning, in fact – before returning to IKEA after the airport shift; the price of sin. At the airport, I removed my jacket and did my best to clean myself up, hoping the night-shift inspector didn't arrive early.

I had the job worked out: I would park my car outside the window of the small office, which was my base for the night, put my bag containing my flask of hot tomato soup and sandwiches on the desk, and switch on my radio. I also had a newspaper and a book to read. Then, I would look around the warehouse for an electric truck, racing around the spaces between the tall shelves – it beat walking; the warehouse was huge. There was a shelf for diplomatic embassy bags, and a place to store the odd coffin in transit; anything which needed to be kept secure. No problem, with me on duty.

Same system as always: keys in strategic places, and my little useless machine. Through the night I drove around, checking and clicking, in between nodding off, with my head on the desk, to briefly wake when I knew the duty inspector was going to arrive, or when I heard his or her car pull up. That was okay in the summer, but snow deadens tyre noise, so more vigilance was required in the winter. When they walked in, I would be the epitome of alertness. Then, once their car lights disappeared, it was head down again and out for the count.

I was armed with a long, rubber truncheon with a lead core, and a gas pistol. The cosh fitted neatly into a special pocket, on the outside of my right trouser-leg, whilst the gas pistol looked like a small gun, with a chamber holding five cartridges; it fitted into a holster at my waist.

I was doing an afternoon shift once, when I popped into the Methodist church, to attend a funeral. I wanted to attend, as the deceased was a man I respected. I parked the Golf outside and wondered if I should take the gun into church. I decided not to and placed it in the glove compartment (from the many films I have seen, people only keep .38s or .45s in glove compartments - never gloves). I entered the church and crept up the stairs at the back, to the gallery. Surely, church galleries were constructed for such circumstances? Well, probably not: they were an overflow, for when churches used to be packed; these days, they are just a useful place to hide the kids, or sneak in late and hide. The gallery was almost empty, though the church was full; the funeral service was well underway.

A young teenager in the gallery seemed mega-impressed with my uniform and leather holster. I guess he imagined there was at least a .38 revolver in the holster, or maybe even a .44 Magnum. More likely a Magnum chocolate ice cream.

The security firm one day got a new manager: a miserable, unpleasant chap, greatly disliked by all. One bright afternoon, he decided that the operatives should all have gas pistol practice – it was of no use or interest to the sales and office staff, just us hard guys. He hung a sack, filled with straw, in an outer building and we lined up.

The idea of using a gas pistol as a defensive weapon is to fire into the aggressor's chest, so the gas drifts upwards into their eyes and nostrils - that's the principle.

We all stood in a line, across the room, and my colleagues each fired off - not bad shooting. Then, my turn came.

The new manager was standing next to the sack, and my aim must have been off, as the gas cartridge hit the sack just beside his head. He started coughing and spluttering, much to the delight of the others; I was a hero - whether by accident or design, I can't remember.

I became involved with mission meetings, in a large tent. I was aware that a week of mission was being arranged outside town, and somehow became involved, preaching on a couple of evenings. This was my first experience of tent meetings and I was impressed - to the point where I am considering arranging them here, in the Calasparra region, some four decades later. All I need is a big tent, but locating a good one in Spain, at the right price, is proving quite a challenge.

During the tent meetings, I met a Norwegian evangelist. Two things he said have made a great impression on me, to this day. One was: "If you are about to be involved in a car crash and you shout *'Jesus!'*, is it a blasphemy or a prayer?" The other has haunted me, throughout my years of ministry: "Are you a pastor or an evangelist?" A simple question, yet puzzlingly profound.

A pastor is a maintainer; the man or woman who leads a congregation, week in week out, whereas an evangelist holds meetings in tents or churches, vigorously proclaiming the Gospel. A maintainer is a teacher to the congregation; an evangelist, like Billy Graham, leads people at specific times, and encourages them to join a church. My experience of evangelists is that they have the gift of inspiring people, through their message. Then, they move on. How can a true evangelist be a pastor?

At that time, I concluded that they are very different ministries; you must be one or the other, but can't be both. I have since battled with this question and arrived at various conclusions. The battle continues.

A maintainer should have pastoral gifts, encourage and teach their congregation - some inspiring, others less so. An evangelist has to be on the ball, steeped in Scripture and always able to inspire; no one books an evangelist who is boring!

Can one person be both? It is possible; churches which are growing enjoy a minister who understands both. Yet, there are frustrations and dangers, which need a prayerful watch, at all times. Why do most middle of the road churches look for pastoral gifts, in their candidates for ordination, but pay less attention to their possible evangelical gifts? High churches do not; their priests are maintainers, whereas low churches see the value of both; Pentecostal churches, also, possibly look for both. What you hope for and what you get are two very different propositions.

When I have arrived at the final answer, I will let you know – but, it won't be on this earth.

CHAPTER EIGHT

Home Again; Home of My Fathers

In 1987, I returned to the U.K. - to my hometown of Blackpool. But, my adventures were far from over; they were only just beginning.

It was low house prices which drew me back to Blackpool. I was in touch with my old principal probation officer, a couple of years before, whilst still living in Norway, and he offered me a job as welfare officer, at an open prison in West Sussex. When he told me the price of even modest houses there, I decided that if I did return to the U.K., it would be to more reasonably priced areas in the north.

Upon my arrival back in Blackpool, a quick browsing of the local newspaper, to scan through the employment ads, and a 'phone call, were followed by an interview the following day. This landed me a job as a social worker, at a local authority home for difficult young teenagers, which also had a secure unit.

I worked in the assessment centre, where boys - who had been sent for various reasons; some by the courts - were to be observed and assessed. There were classrooms and dormitory accommodation - all locked. The home provided a house for me to rent on campus, but when I first arrived, in the late evening, I was placed in a cell for the night, though they did not lock the door.

I found it difficult to work out who were the most psychologically disturbed there: the boys or the staff. The head had alcohol problems, whilst his deputy was a very strange man, who listened at doors and, when the head was absent, would spend his time trying to fish documents out of the head's locked desk drawer, with a letter opener. Knowing this, the head had put a note in his drawer one day, before he went away, stating: "Waste of time, xxxxxx. Nothing of interest here!"

There were teachers who took daily classes. Many seemed to be misfits in the educational system, if not society as a whole; the woodwork teacher was eventually suspended, for his physical assaults on pupils. A strict regime ruled throughout. I witnessed one boy being told to make his bed, then the whole mattress being thrown to the floor, with an order to remake it - much to the amusement of the staff present.

I survived a year or so in this environment of social misfits (mainly the staff) before going to work in the same local authority, as a children and family social worker. This introduced me to the area of child protection, which was to become my future career. I studied, at night-school, for a Post-16 Certificate in Education, and for some time was a trainer in child protection, and a lead trainer for a county council. They say "when you can't do it any more, teach it", but in no way did that apply to me: I moved from training to being a children's guardian, and representing their interests in care proceedings: getting them a barrister; meeting them in family courts, with local authority barristers, parents' barristers and whoever else was a party to the proceedings; and, finally preparing a detailed court report, advising the judge on the applicable order(s).

It was during these years that I passed through various "religious phases".

I had been baptized and confirmed in the Church of England, and at fifteen I became a local Methodist preacher, remaining a Methodist for some thirty years. In Norway, I had attended the Seventh-Day Adventist Church, which I read about in a pamphlet, which arrived in my post box (no letter boxes in Norway, because of the winter snow; post is delivered to rows of post boxes near one's house). As I read it, I thought how interesting this hitherto unknown denomination seemed. I attended local evening meetings in the town, and was baptized in an Adventist Church. I had long been in conflict about baby baptism, the state of the dead and Heaven, and as I watched an Adventist minister unfolding their beliefs with a Powerpoint presentation, I found myself ticking off, in my head, all the similarities Adventists have to what I believed at that time. I also attended Pentecostal and Baptist churches, to find out more about their beliefs, and I will never regret investigating this.

There are so many differing beliefs in Christianity. For example, Saturday is their Sabbath, and I became very interested in their reasoning for this. I decided that no one holds all of the truth; it is shared. Looking on *Wikipedia*, I see that the list of Protestant denominations is mind-blowing, and very confusing.

Adventist churches in Norway have quite large congregations, mainly made up of professionals. So, when I searched for a Seventh-Day Adventist church in Blackpool, I was surprised to find only a small congregation, with under ten regular members. The minister served two churches: Blackpool and Preston. The latter was much larger, with roughly a hundred members, who were almost entirely of West Indian background.

I learnt much when I preached at the Preston church - particularly their commitment. Services would start with Bible study, which could last for a couple of hours; the formal service afterward had no time limit. Then, at a Jacob's join communal lunch, everyone would provide at least one dish. The Preston church often went out into their community, spreading information about the church, and holding evangelical services in public places. It was a wonderful fellowship.

One Saturday afternoon, I found myself preaching on a packed Preston market square, supported by a fantastic West Indian choir and a group of talented musicians. The church leaders asked me to preach. At the appropriate moment I stepped forward, microphone in hand. The crowd seemed vast, and interested. I spoke about the French philosopher Jean-Jacques Rousseau saying 'Man is born free and everywhere he is in chains'. As I was developing this thought, I saw out of the corner of my eye a young man staggering towards me from the crowd.

He came right up to me, grabbed the microphone, muttered 'Daisy chains' and staggered back into the crowd. At least he had been listening.

Get out of that one Andrew! I said something about the young man recalling his experience of daisy chains and moved quickly on, thankful that the drug addict did not wish to expand on his philosophy!

Another Saturday afternoon I was outside the Marks and Spencer store, in Blackpool. I will never forget seeing people sitting nearby on benches, applauding - though I was never sure whether it was for my words, the music, or both.

In the Church of England, there are congregations for the very high, high, middle of the road, low and very low traditions - I have always considered this their greatest strength and their greatest weakness. How difficult must it be to be the Archbishop of Canterbury, having to hold it all together, not just in the U.K., but across the world, in the Anglican Communion? I have attended a few Roman Catholic churches in England and Spain, and have often reflected on the uniformity of their belief and services. At least, in bygone days.

CHAPTER NINE

Into the Wilderness

I then entered what I can only describe as a spiritual wilderness, though it was probably only for a few months. My faith remained strong, but I was unsure which denomination to follow.

My Anglican roots are in the low church tradition: no calling the vicar "Father", or going to Confession - Heaven forbid.

It is said that we are all products of our upbringing, and I feel that this applies to how we follow our Christian faith - or any religion, for that matter. Being a natural-born rebel, I wanted to find out for myself. It is interesting that when I was looking for a Church of England, I walked into a low church.

It was time to return to my Anglican roots. Not sure how this occurred, but I started to attend a Church of England church, opposite where I was living. I was driving past my house, one Sunday afternoon, when I felt *called* to attend this church, or to put it specifically, an inner voice was saying: *Get into that church!* I did so, though found it to be just another station, along the track on my journey of faith, not the destination. I stayed in this church for a year or so, where I attended and hosted a fellowship group.

Then came the next stage. I was driving along an arterial road in Blackpool, when, outside a Church of England church, I saw a large poster, which boldly stated: *"Seven days without prayer makes one WEAK"*. I liked to read this wayside pulpit, which changed weekly - the traffic lights up ahead were always on red, so I had the time. One Sunday morning I went in, where I received a warm welcome; the vicar understood the importance of enlisting a team of lay-people, to make a beeline for newcomers to the congregation.

This church was my Waterloo: it was here that I was put forward for ordination into the Church of England. Over the years, I had felt called to ordained ministry several times - starting on that Christmas morning, at the age of nine. The feeling continued into my teens, coming to a head at the age of twenty-three, whilst studying to be a probation officer, when I talked with a Methodist minister. It was he who felt that working in social work and as a local preacher may be my calling - probably wise advice at the time.

When I was in Norway, I was taken under the wing of a Methodist minister who organised mission work for the Norwegian Methodist Church. He was the one who sent me to Argentina, and who, upon my return, was supportive, should I wish to apply for ordination, in the Methodist Church. I decided not to pursue that possibility, but I did fly to London, to see the Bishop of Gibraltar - now the Diocese of Europe. I found his apartment and walked up the stairs, into a large lounge. He had a manservant who reminded me of Lurch, of *The Addams Family*: creeping in silently, holding a tray laden with tea and scones. The bishop told me that his neighbour was Dinah Sheridan - the actress who had starred in the film *Genevieve*, with Kenneth More. I have never quite worked out the relevance of this information, during a preliminary interview for ordination, but I looked suitably impressed, I suppose. We chatted about this and that for some time, then I left.

I received a letter from an aide, a week later in Norway, saying that I would not be considered for ordination. I believe it was because I had met with a canon at Charing Cross Station, who was Director of Ordinands for the Diocese, and had told him I was low church. To which he replied: "Well, perhaps you should apply to the Methodist Church, then," before he promptly disappeared.

I had returned to Norway disheartened and confused. I had been naïve, trusting in those whom I considered to be important in the Church, and that they knew what they were doing.

Still, I was going back to live in the U.K., anyway, so I just had to get on with life as a lay minister; ordination was clearly not for me...

Oh, I almost forgot of an incident in a Norwegian graveyard, during which I sat on a bench all night, praying and looking at the dark skyline. After several hours, I decided to make a deal with God: if a light appeared in the sky, I would take that as a sign for ordination. I waited and waited. A light did finally appear (though, on reflection, it was probably an aeroplane), so off I went, the following morning, to see the Methodist minister. He didn't like me. Creep. He was unimpressed with my night vigil and would not take me seriously. Thank the Lord...

When I returned to Blackpool, I put such thoughts out of my mind, telling myself to get on with my life, help people in my daily work and enjoy a lay ministry.

Then came the spiritual wilderness experience and life outside of organized religion. I felt free, but no inner peace.

One evening, I was out for a walk, when suddenly this thought hit me, like a brick from the sky: *Get ordained.* Oh, yeah? Thanks very much, but no thanks: been there; got the T-shirt. But, the feeling would not go away. By this time, I was attending the Church of England – the one with the wayside pulpit - and allowed to preach at regular intervals. I approached the vicar and he invited me into his study, where, to my amazement, he seemed interested and thought that I had a genuine call to ordination. I was so nervous, I had to leave his study several times and retreat to the loo next door.

I was sent to be interviewed by three separate bishops. At the first of the trilogy, the bishop asked me if I had completed the necessary application form for ordination. Feeling that he was going to reject me, I replied that I had the form, but I kept kicking it in the dust, underneath my desk. He was confused and sent me to see another bishop.

On the day of the second interview, I was in court in the morning, representing a child in care proceedings. I collected my new car, from the car park underneath the court, and as I was reversing out, I hit a concrete post, knocking off the driver's wing mirror and denting the door. I surveyed the damage, angry at myself for being so careless, then I drove to see the bishop. As I stopped, by a park behind his house, I was deep in thought: surely the damage was a sign, and not a good one. Or, was it Satan, perhaps, trying to discourage me?

I rang the doorbell and the bishop greeted me cordially. He made coffee, and whilst he was out of the room, I glanced at one of the many books in his bookcase on Benedictines - this was obviously his thing. He questioned me with rapier-like incisions. I managed to answer them, as best I could, even slipping in a comment I had managed to skim from one of his books; brownie points! It seemed to go down well; fortunately, we didn't have time for him to explore any deep thoughts I might have on the subject matter. The bishop wrote a positive report on our encounter, and recommended that I be given further consideration as a candidate for ordination.

At my interview with the Diocesan Bishop, he told me that ordination candidates from his diocese, who proceeded to selection conference, were always successful. No pressure there, then! He then put me forward to selection conference: a weekend of tests and interviews.

I had changed my car for a much cheaper model, by this time, and as I pulled into the car park for the conference, the water temperature gauge was in the red: radiator leak. Another sign from the other side, that this was all just a waste of time?

The chair of the conference had actually smiled and nodded, as I explained why I felt called to ordination. I made the statement that I felt called to work with homosexuals, and possibly start a church for them, because they have been so neglected. The chairman seemed very interested, and kept nodding as I spoke.

And, somehow, I passed the tests and interviews. I was on my way.

I studied part-time, for three years, which meant attending evening tutorials, residential training for one weekend every month and summer courses. I was ordained as a deacon, and a year later, as a priest.

My diocesan bishop, who was fairly new in post, was very encouraging and supportive. He seemed to see something worthwhile in me, and I have deep affection and respect for him. Through the years, I have met a good number of ministers, priests and bishops, with varying experiences, and I considered this bishop a true man of God.

After ordination, I served as an N.S.M. (Non-Stipendiary Minister) curate, which meant that I earnt my living from Monday to Saturday, and worked for free for the Church, in the evenings and on Sundays.

Then, when my wife and I moved to Spain to retire (?), I served for four years in the Anglican Chaplaincy of Torrevieja.

CHAPTER TEN

Back to the Beginning

From here on in, I will try to describe *The Road to Calasparra: The Promised Land*. This was originally to be the title of this book, but as I started to write, so much of my life and ministry seemed relevant in setting the scene, so *Holy Inadequate* seems much more appropriate.

They say "what goes around comes around" – well, I have been round and round, in seemingly ever-decreasing circles, yet feel it was all preparation for my ministry today. Without all of my varied experience, I would be much poorer. True, there are some things I would have done differently - some *very* differently – but that's life: we win some; we lose some. We should accept the past and the lessons learnt, but not dwell on it. Use the wisdom gained to live in the present and look to the future.

After that Sunday afternoon in La Marina, it seemed that there was only one way forward: to find land for the retreat.

I am friends with the man who looked after the congregation at La Manga Club, a golf complex with great sports facilities. He runs an estate agency business, and I rang him to ask if he knew of any land for sale in Murcia. This is a large and beautiful area of Spain, where my understanding was that land prices are reasonable. He replied that he didn't know of any land, but would make enquiries and let me know.

A couple of months later, I received a call back from him, telling me that a man who lives in Yorkshire was selling his land, in Calasparra, Murcia.

"Where? Never heard of it!"

The reply was that the land would be perfect for a retreat: it was near Caravaca de la Cruz, one of the holy centres of the world. I went on the internet and sought information. Turned out they grow rice, marked "Produced in Calasparra", which it seems one can buy in any U.K. supermarket. I'd always imagined a bunch of Chinese guys, wearing coolies, working in rice fields.

I got directions to the land - three adjoining plots - and Jean and I set off to find it. We must have missed the plots by one road, so the next day we returned - and found it.

It was perfect for a retreat, surrounded by hills of peace and quiet, yet not isolated. The town of Calasparra was just a few minutes' drive away; neighbours, but not on the doorstep.

Two of the large plots were adjacent and the third crossed a small, rural lane, with a total area of just over ten-thousand square metres. Two plots were olive groves, but the smallest was open land, ready to be built on without expensive preparation; perfect for the retreat. We knew the size was important, as every council in Spain seems to have its own different requirements for building permission. When the Yorkshireman gained planning permission to build two houses on the plots in 2005, the land requirement was five-thousand square metres per plot. This was later changed to ten thousand, and by now could have even been twenty thousand.

Negotiations commenced.

I was concerned about dealing with a Yorkshireman, but my friend helped us arrive at what was a very acceptable deal. We bought the land and signed the documentation on the 5th November 2015 (the date and significance giving me some humorous concern: would it all blow up in my face?).

Calasparra is about an hour and fifteen minutes drive from La Marina, mainly on motorways (which are only two lanes in Spain), so we looked for a caravan. We found one, advertised by an elderly German couple who had lived in it for several years, on a small, permanent site, but were now returning home. It was large, with an end bedroom and awning, and when we saw it the large awning was decked out, as one would expect for a static home. It also had a domestic fridge-freezer and a full-size cooker. A sideboard, laden with ornaments, and a proper door into the awning, had been made by the German guy, who was very handy with such things.

It was perfect for us to live in, as we planned the next phase. After talking to friends, about leaving it on their land for the interim (they lived close to where it was for sale, and had land around their home), we bought it.

The problem now was how to transport the caravan. It was too heavy for my car to tow even the eight kilometres to their house, let alone the hundred and thirty kilometres to Calasparra. A friend offered to tow it with his 4x4 and "take a chance", knowing that if he was stopped by a Guardia Civil traffic patrol there would be questions about his towing a caravan of that size, and his insurance. But, I resisted the offer, and looked on the internet for legal local towing firms. I finally found an Englishman with an American monster truck. He did a good job of towing the caravan from the site to our friends' house, and we parked it there for a couple of months, until we were ready to move it to Calasparra.

Our first job was to fence off the retreat land. Our estate agent friend introduced us to a building firm in Calasparra, and their agent spoke fairly good English. His boss, however - who was often abroad, doing projects - did not, and when I managed to speak with him, he was offhand and unhelpful. Eventually, and at great cost, a two-metre high, metal fence was erected around the land, with space for a four-metre-wide gate.

The day for our move to Calasparra arrived. We met the tow-truck man and, after watching him hitch up the caravan, led him off. All went well, with us in front and him following; along roads, and on two motorways - no problems and no Guardia Civil. As far as I was concerned, the guy had relevant insurance, and certainly a sturdy enough vehicle.

When we approached our land, I realized that a big swing was required by long vehicles, to drive through the gates. The lane was narrow, but there was room to swing out, over the neighbour's land, opposite the four-metre gap. The monster truck was about three metres long, and the caravan another six, including the tow bar. Tight, but do-able… just.

I stood in the lane and directed the towing guy, but he had already driven through the gate entrance and onto the land, and was out of hearing distance. On reflection, I would have been better standing in front of him and directing from there, rather than standing in the lane behind.

He swung the truck in and the caravan followed – unfortunately, scraping and bending a metal gate post, and smashing a lounge window on that side. When he finally stopped and jumped out, I had to point out the damage, of which he was blissfully unaware. Surveying it, he commented that I could get a replacement window on the internet. I was just thankful that we hadn't had the accident on a motorway, or broken down anywhere.

And, even more thankful when he manoeuvred the vehicle back and forth, into the corner of the land where I wanted the caravan. That was until we unhitched the caravan and it started to roll down the incline, towards where the gate would be, gathering speed. We managed to halt it, before further damage could occur, by standing at the back and using our shoulders as buffers. Thankfully, it stopped. Handbrake on, rocks under the double wheels, and home at last!

I wanted a sliding gate, but the arrogant boss told me that this was not possible, as the land sloped. I insisted.

I was on a visit to see my eye specialist in Torrevieja, as we had not yet moved our medical care to Calasparra, when I received a worried telephone call from Jean, to say that two workmen were mixing concrete for the gate, and it all looked a mess.

I drove back as quickly as possible, to find two guys and a heap of concrete. And, I mean a *heap*, spread roughly along the four metres where the gate runner was going. They were mixing the concrete by hand, but even I know that an electric mixer is required for building work, and that concrete is delivered on a lorry, for larger developments, mixing as it drives along. Still, they laid it reasonably smoothly, with wheelbarrows and spades and, by the time they departed, I could just about envisage the runner for the sliding gate.

Some time later two men arrived, to erect a two-metre-high fence around the plot. They did good, speedy work, though they were expensive. Finally, a firm came to put on the sliding gate.

It worked well, though it was manual, and not a remote-controlled electric gate, which would have been far too expensive. The only problem was that the gate was open metal, so anyone passing could see through it - not ideal for a peaceful retreat centre. The metal fencing, too, was open to the world.

My next mistake was due to ignorance.

Out of the blue, a couple of gypsy men turned up and offered to put cane onto the fence, along the side which was open to the lane and the passing cars. Additionally, they would put bundles of wooden strips onto the gate. They showed me photos of bar-table umbrellas, which they had allegedly constructed.

Never give your Whatsapp details to people you don't know!

I did, and during the following days, I received countless messages in Spanish, demanding to know if I was interested.

We finally agreed a price and the work was done.

I had previously been advised not to use plastic sheets for screening on the fencing, as the wind can blow it away. Well, cane has the same effect, if laid double, like ours was: the wind cannot get through, the screening acting like a sail. But, a single row does not provide much privacy. Anyway, the fencing at the front blew down a couple of times, until eventually the cane had to be removed, and replaced with what looks like plastic grass – it was recommended by our builder, and it works. Unless cats start playing on the top of it, that is: then, it droops.

CHAPTER ELEVEN

A Serious Problem

We had not lived in the caravan for long, when Jean was diagnosed with colon cancer.

We hadn't had time to move our medical care from La Marina to Calasparra, and were still registered with Torrevieja Hospital, which has a good international reputation. I remember, when we met the surgeon in his office at the hospital, staring at his feet: old, suede Chelsea boots. I was fascinated by them, my gaze moving up to the screen, then back again. Those feet still haunt me.

He explained, in English, that Jean had colon cancer, and showed us on the computer screen. He told us he would do his best to ensure that she would not need a colostomy bag. It was a big shock for both of us, but I think Jean took it more stoically than me.

Then started the drive up and down the motorway - an hour and a half each way. Waiting for the tests, the anaesthetist, the surgeon, and the operation date... It was only a few weeks, before there we were: sitting in a room, with a nurse getting Jean prepared.

I went up to a waiting area, which had a detailed, electronic screen. When the patient's name and date of birth were entered, information about the procedure of the operation came up, including finish time and the room she would be taken to for recovery, then where she would stay until discharge.

The health system in Spain is excellent, and free of charge – ex-pats in Spain are assured that Brexit will make no difference. I cynically joke that Spain wants us all to stay and spend our pensions, rather than sell our houses, which would be major financial loss for them. Besides, the U.K. government will not want thousands of ex-pats flooding back, putting an extra drain on the N.H.S. and housing system. We know where we are wanted - and appreciated...

I kept anxiously checking the screen: "Operation in progress"... "Operation completed"... "Taken to recovery"...

I ran out of the waiting room to find the surgeon, and met him on the stairs, which I guessed he was climbing to come and see me. As I looked into his face, from the steps above, he said: "No problem; everything went well. No bag!" I wanted to hug him!

I waited outside the single room, with an appointed bathroom, and was so pleased to see Jean being wheeled from a lift, in her bed. She was conscious and seemed okay. There was even a bed for me to sleep on - a sofa which folded out - and bedding. I stayed with her overnight, and for all of the following days, until discharge. Unfortunately, soon after the operation, she developed vertigo and was sick. When the surgeon came to see her, the following morning, he ordered that she be taken, still in the bed, to be examined by a specialist. She was treated and rapidly improved.

Each day, I sat for long periods in the car (no hospital parking charges in Spain), emailing friends in Spain and relatives in the U.K. about Jean's progress.

Finally, discharge day arrived, along with an appointment to see an oncologist at the hospital. Eight sessions of chemotherapy were booked, but she would not lose her hair. So, the treatment started.

After the first session, I was helping her to the lift, when she became dizzy and faint. I got her back into the chemo ward and nurses checked her out. She was immediately wheeled down to an emergency room, where it was thought that she'd had a stroke. A subsequent scan showed that this was not the case, but rather a reaction to the drugs. What a great relief! After a couple more hours she was discharged, and we set off to the caravan.

Chemotherapy is not pleasant at any time, but when living in a caravan, in forty degrees, it is most unpleasant.

A few months earlier our builder friend had given us a puppy - an Alsatian and Podenco (Spanish hunting dog) cross, which we called Zeba - and this faithful friend lay on her bunk next to Jean, all the time.

Zeba stayed with us for two and a half years, watching us move from the caravan to the cabin, then into the house - a constant companion. Just before Christmas 2018 she passed away, from what we think was a genetic kidney problem, as we were later told that one of her brothers in the litter had also died.

Zeba was an angel. She comforted Jean and us both, and would walk the land with me, on long, hot nights, as I shouted at the sky: "Why?" Later, she would walk around the house with me on many mornings, at 4 a.m., as I struggled to come to terms with an intransient Church of England.

With tears of immense sorrow and deep gratitude we buried Zeba on the land, underneath a young olive tree. An angel sent to help us both through a most difficult time, her work was now done, and she departed. There are tears in my eyes as I write this, seven months on.

Still, we had to go on. The next job was getting the water and electricity connected.

We became friendly with our neighbour, Sebastian; we see him most days, as he keeps racing pigeons in a large shed, which he visits daily, throughout the year, to feed and look after. He and his wife have a flat in the centre of Calasparra, but in the summer months they live in a house next to the retreat plot.

In winter, the two solar panels I had put behind the caravan for electricity were not charging the 12-volt battery in the caravan (which, via an inverter, supplied 220v of electricity), so Sebastian let me plug into the electricity supply in his pigeon shed.

He also allowed us to fill up eight-litre water bottles, with a hosepipe from his pigeon shed. Having to fill the caravan water tank with heavy bottles filled by hosepipe was not ideal: most of the water was used for showers, which my wife needed, as the chemotherapy treatment caused her much discomfort. So, I would stand naked under a hosepipe on the land, showering. No problem in the summer, but most unpleasant in winter: contrary to opinion in the U.K., Spanish winters can be cold, and in the Calasparra region there was even some snow. This is why ex-pat Brits object so strongly to losing our Winter Heating Allowance, when living in Spain, because U.K. politicians assume that we live in hot weather throughout the year.

Sebastian knew where the water pipe ran underneath the lane – or, he *thought* he did. So, we asked a Spanish builder, who had been recommended by an English couple, to dig up the lane. What a circus!

As we peered into the big hole in the lane, with the guy standing next to us, we heard several comments from him to Sebastian: "No hay agua." *("No water"*!). Sebastian then went on to tell us that the only man who knew the layout of the water pipes had recently passed away. Just my luck!

After some probing in the hole the water pipe was located. The builder connected to the main, and ran a pipe into the plot. Now we had water, via an outside tap, to which we could connect a hosepipe.

To my great consternation, they then all disappeared for a siesta, leaving a gaping hole - two metres deep and a metre across - halfway across the lane, with no warning signs. I had visions of people driving up the lane, in either direction, and the front of their car or scooter disappearing into it! With my luck, the responsibility would be mine. The next day, the builder filled in the hole, much to my relief.

In order to live with some permanence in Spain, when buying land to build on, there are two necessities to consider: how available is water, and is there electricity connection available? One does not want a petrol generator running, twelve hours a day, to supply electricity. Initially, I got the T-shirt for that one, too. Water sorted; now electricity.

I got to know an electrician who lived down the lane, and he gave me estimates for a supply, from an electricity company, and one for solar panels. The latter seemed like a good idea in Spain, for obvious reasons. What put me off was the cost, and the number of large solar panels which would need to be put on the land. I also had doubts about how long the batteries would last before requiring replacement - I was told approximately ten years. Remember, I was asking questions and trying to understand the answers in my limited Spanish; misunderstandings do occur. After much thought, I decided to get an electricity supply.

Two large pillars would need erecting, for the supply to go from a pillar by the electrician's house: one on a neighbour's plot and one on our land. Our architect contacted the owner of a corner plot to enquire about the cost of erecting a pillar: two thousand euros! My expression on hearing the price must have said it all, because the architect said he had another idea. He got in touch with a local farmer, who owned the land by the electrician's house, and came back to say that we could erect a pillar on his land for nothing. So, an overhead electricity cable would be run from the pillar next to the electrician's house, for a few metres, to a pillar on the farmer's land, then to one on our plot. The cost (apart from the electrician's work, which was good, but not cheap) was a card of gratitude and a couple of bottles of spirits and chocolates, for the farmer and his family.

It all worked out very well. The two pillars were erected and the cables connected. An electricity meter was put in concrete housing, at the foot of the pillar on our land, then an underground trench was dug from the meter, right through our two plots, to the retreat, providing electricity for our future house and the retreat.

We had just moved into our new house, when there was an electricity blackout; a guy working outside with a digger had cut the underground cable, claiming that the builder had not told him how deep the trench was, and that the electrician had not told the builder. They all speak Spanish, for goodness' sake…

I rang the builder, and he promptly arrived with his own electrician. After various telephone calls, by the builder to the electricity company, it appeared that something had been blown in their equipment, by the damage to the underground cable. Yet, to my amazement, the supply recommenced that evening. Something to be said for siesta time: workers knock off at 2 p.m., start again about 5 p.m. and work until 8 p.m.

We got ripped off by a couple of Brit builders, while we were living in the caravan, and Jean was still receiving chemo, after her operation - not pleasant at any time, but particularly gruelling in a caravan, with few amenities and temperatures in the early forties. I was desperate to move her into a comfortable, wooden cabin, and was recommended by a friend to consult a local British builder. I don't think he had undertaken such a large project as building a cabin from scratch, so I tried him out on a couple of small projects, and his carpentry work seemed okay; he started well.

We agreed a price, complete with plumbing and electrical work in his estimate, and agreed a time scale. This was all done on Whatsapp; nothing in writing and no contract. Also, no receipts for materials purchased. Silly me. My only excuse is that my head was in turmoil, and Jean promptly needed to be moved to more comfortable accommodation. I kept transferring money into his local bank account, whenever he asked. When he needed money to repair his car, alarm bells sounded, but still I paid up.

The crunch came when it became obvious that he did not know how to do the roof, and the agreed completion date had now passed by two months. The roof was tiled, but was unfinished and did not look safe; the cabin structure, which was just a wooden shell, did not seem to support it properly. I finally asked him to leave. I'd already had to pay the plumber for his work. That left us minus about six-thousand euros on the project, which I know we will not see again.

By now I was in deep despair. We were visiting a friend near Torrevieja, when a man who was changing his front-door lock overheard our conversation about the cabin. He had built wooden buildings in Texas, and I think he even mentioned chapels. Was this God speaking? The solution to all my current problems? He said he would drive up and take a look at the cabin, with a British architect.

He did so, and duly pronounced that the cabin was unsafe.

He said he would finish the cabin and build a wooden chapel, for the cost of the materials only. This was music to my ears.

Again, all started well, but before long I was paying for his labour, as well as materials. Still, the cabin was completed, and the materials arrived to build the chapel.

I asked my Spanish builder to safely complete the cabin's roof, which he did at very little cost. He had become a friend, when he completed several small jobs on the land, and in fact built our lovely brick house, on the land next to the retreat - to estimate and a high standard. He even gave us Zeba, who was from his bitch's litter.

Money, money, money! Our careful resources began to dwindle, at a rate of knots.

But, Jean was improving rapidly, thanks to the excellent Spanish healthcare system - all paid for from the U.K., where we had both paid in through the years.

The next crunch came when the British guy offered to build us a wooden house. He gave an estimate, but later I discovered that the likely final cost was going to be about the same as a traditional brick house. By this time, the chapel was constructed, at double the estimated cost.

Wooden buildings are treated with some suspicion in Spain, and wood is expensive - very different from Norway. I signed a contract to build a wooden house for us, but with an important clause: we would pay a deposit, but it was refundable, if we did not receive permission from the local council to build in wood. Then, I consulted our architect: a helpful, young, local lad, just qualified. In effect, he said: "No way, Jose; you won't get planning permission for a wooden house."

When I asked for our 8,700€ deposit back, I was told: "Financial difficulties." What about *our* financial difficulties, trying to exist on our pensions? As well as having to take two bank loans, just to cover the monies owed to us.

The guy repaid in small monthly instalments, which didn't even cover our loan repayments. When he had repaid a total of 1,000€, they stopped: "health problems" and "difficulty finding work".

So, there we are. Or, rather, *here* we are: hard lessons painfully learnt. Moral of the story? Don't let your head be overcome by your heart; whenever possible, use a Spanish builder in Spain. Oh, not all Brit builders are dishonest and not all Spanish builders are honest - far from it - but…

CHAPTER TWELVE

So, here we are...

As I have said, I was an associate priest in the Chaplaincy of St. Peter and St. Paul, Torrevieja, for four years, with a Permission to Officiate (PTO) from the Diocese of Europe, Church of England.

Forty years rolled by, before I started writing again. *Regrets, I've had a few...* I mention it now, as I *do* have regrets. Time was never on my side. Well, that's my excuse... to myself.

When I was in the Chaplaincy of St. Peter and St. Paul life was at last relaxed enough to write a couple of stage comedies. I formed a drama group called "The Chaplaincy Players", and was the writer (well, more correctly the *co*-writer, as my good friend Alec Winwood worked with me on the first script), also producing, directing and starring in both which were produced at the same local theatre.

The first was entitled *Make Believe*, produced in 2014, and was a comedy about a unmarried, naïve new priest in the Chaplaincy, and his attempts to ward off the attention of some rather amorous ladies, and included a humorous pair of sisters, called Chummy and Bunny, who brought the house down. They were chalk and cheese, both in stature and personality. The real-life Chummy has recently passed away, leaving very fond memories of a memorable onstage performance.

Alec has also passed on, though when writing I sometimes feel his presence over my shoulder, muttering: "You can't say that!"

The second, which I wrote alone, was entitled *Knockin' on Heaven's Door*. It was produced in 2015, about the residents of a care home in the

U.K., who constantly plotted against the matron, who ruled with a rod of iron.

The same cast played in both productions and we had great fun. We rehearsed in a room at a local restaurant, hamming up both scripts with creative joy. I felt that it brought members of the Chaplaincy together, other than on Sunday mornings and social events, and showed that Christians can enjoy themselves.

All good things come to an end, some more tragically than others. The Chaplaincy Players met its end through money, the profits from the first production going 100% into Chaplaincy funds. As a drama group, we decided that the profit from the second should be equally divided between the Chaplaincy and two charities, including one for the homeless.

I remember sitting at a Chaplaincy Council meeting, being humiliated by the treasurer, as he listed requirements The Chaplaincy Players should adhere to, if they wanted to remain under the Chaplaincy. We decided not to, and disbanded, with deep frustration and regret. I could not believe that something so light-hearted and innocent could be so viciously attacked, simply because we wanted to share our hard-earned profit with two local charities. When we gave all the profit from the first production to Chaplaincy funds, there was no mention of restrictions, but when we did not give all the profit from the second production to the Chaplaincy, massive obstacles were suddenly placed in our path, should we wish to continue. Surely, churches should be sharing some of their income with charities, simply to be worthy of the name.

During this unfortunate period the Chaplaincy was in an Interregnum, the previous fair-minded chaplain having left, and his replacement awaited. When the future of The Chaplaincy Players was discussed, the chair of the Chaplaincy Council was a lay-person who, in my opinion, did not have the experience or wisdom to step in and prevent the onslaught I endured, following the second production. Had the chair been the previous chaplain, the result might not have been so destructive.

When we moved to Calasparra it seemed natural to still be a part of the Chaplaincy, and the Chaplaincy Council unanimously agreed. I count myself unfortunate that the chaplain changed just as we moved. The previous chaplain was a man I got on with and respected, during my four years in Chaplaincy ministry; his successor was a different sort of man.

At first, he seemed supportive, and we brought him to see the land, before we moved. He never came again, but when the congregation started, he was controlling of the services I conducted – and, very concerned about the amount received in collections from the congregation. I sent him monthly reports, always seeking to respect the trust my P.T.O. and the Chaplaincy had placed in me.

When I received an email, saying that I should talk to my congregation about their low financial giving, it was the last straw. Several of the congregation gave in kind; one couple bought chairs and cushions for the chapel, among other items; one provided a large television, which I wanted to use as a screen for hymns and the weekly order of service, instead of books; one man helps me to keep the weeds down, and has built a sign for the retreat, as well as other things. I felt it was an insult to say that people were not putting enough cash in the plate. We did not take collections during the services, but there was a plate at the back, should they wish to donate on their way out. Weekly donations were, in my opinion, very reasonable.

I decided I wanted to leave the Chaplaincy, but I knew this could be a problem. As an Anglican priest, I must have Episcopal oversight; in Spain, non-Roman Catholic denominations should be registered with FEREDE (Federacion de Entidades Religiosas Evangelicas de Espana), which is part of the Ministry of Justice. This has always been something of a mystery to me, although I understand that the Church of England is registered with FEREDE, because I hold an identity card with my photograph, should anyone ask to see it. No-one ever has. I also knew that the worship centres of the Chaplaincy - mostly R.C. churches, rented for services - were registered. I was mostly concerned about whether services I conducted in the chapel also needed to be registered.

There followed months of sleepless nights and my pacing, first in the cabin, then later the house, with faithful Zeba. How could I legally conduct Anglican services in the chapel? And, should the retreat be registered with FEREDE?

When the Suffragan Bishop of Europe visited the Chaplaincy, to conduct confirmations, Jean and I asked for a meeting. We met with him at the chaplain's house and I explained that I wished to leave the Chaplaincy. His reaction was that I must then resign my Holy Orders. It was clear that if my ministry was not under the supervision of the chaplain, then I would not be permitted (or trusted) to serve independently with a P.T.O. It was a shock, as was the fact that the bishop never offered to pray with us. We knew he had a flight to catch back to the U.K., and time was of the essence, but I have never met with a bishop who has not offered a prayer.

What should I do now? Go it alone, outside the Anglican Communion, conducting services and inviting people to the retreat? I wanted everything to be above board and legal, and this was foremost in my mind, as I paced, night after night, and prayed.

A good friend, who we met through my monthly articles in a Murcia magazine entitled *The Rockin' Vicar*, was a great support and help. He is a Roman Catholic, who lives in Ireland and has a holiday home on the Spanish coast. We first met when he was in Spain; he came to visit us at the retreat and we became firm friends. He has wonderful knowledge of churches and knows some very interesting people. He put me in touch with an Anglican priest in the U.K., who had similar problems with the Church of England.

We spoke on the 'phone and emailed each other for a while, and whilst his advice was sound, it was unproductive. My opinion was that the Suffragan Bishop's mind was made up, and that this filtered down to the archdeacon and, of course, the chaplain. I was, and still am, unaware of the chaplain's role in the Church's attitude to my ministry.

Our Irish friend then put me in touch with an Anglican bishop who had resigned from the Church of England, and joined an Anglican church in America. We spoke on the telephone and by Skype.

He said he was soon to be the Bishop for Europe on behalf of the American Church, and would be happy for me to join his small group of clergy, disaffected with the Church of England. But, on investigating the beliefs of the American Church and the bishop, it became clear that their beliefs are not my beliefs. I could bite the bullet and throw my battered hat into their ring, but I felt this would be hypocritical; a means to an end.

Sleepless nights became weeks and months. Was this the end of the road? Or, should I take the "illegal" road and hang the consequences, if any? I have always been a risk-taker. My decades in child protection sometimes caused concern, because I supported parents and families whom the system dismissed. One dear diocesan bishop apparently told people that he saw my ability to take risks as a strength; he always prayed with me, even when I had crossed the line, and supported and encouraged me through a very dark time.

Then our Irish friend, Gerry, told me about the Episcopal Church of Spain, headed by Bishop Dr. Carlos Lopez Lozano, in the Anglican Communion, headed by the Archbishop of Canterbury. Was this the answer?

I found out as much information as possible about the Church and liked what I read. I contacted Bishop Carlos and he drove the three-hundred-odd kilometres from Madrid, in his battered, ageing Skoda, to meet me in Calasparra. We sat in the chapel and I went through my list of questions. His English is very good, and he has ministered in the States and the U.K. He not only answered all of my questions, but provided information, including that he is on the board of FEREDE!

I was mega-impressed with the man - my idea of what a bishop should be, and a guy I could do business with. At long last! He was impressed with our endeavours to start a retreat. He prayed in Spanish and I in English - the sweetest prayers of hope.

When I asked in what capacity I might fit into his Church, Bishop Carlos immediately replied as a priest, with his licence; he considered a P.T.O. to be second class. Wow! I would be the Vicar of Calasparra! With no more worries, protected on all sides: from above, and by the Episcopal Church of Spain. Awesome. All those months of worry, all the enquiries and planning, and now the answer was staring me in the face.

I took Bishop Carlos at his word; we had done a deal.

After the euphoria settled, I started wondering: had I dreamt it all? Had I misunderstood? Had *he* misunderstood? Would he indeed give me his licence? If so, when?

A couple of days after his visit, I emailed him to say that I would conduct a service of Morning Worship that coming Sunday, with no Holy Communion: I cannot do an Anglican Eucharist or Holy Communion without Episcopal oversight. When he replied, he seemed rather surprised: of course I could conduct a Eucharistic service.

Oh well, I thought, *stop the doubting Thomas stuff and get stuck in.*

So, that's what I did, and I have never looked back.

Four months after our first meeting, Bishop Carlos arrived in

Calasparra on a Sunday morning, to conduct my induction as a priest in his Church, responsible for Calasparra church. The chapel was packed, including many friends from the Chaplaincy. During the service, he officially presented me with my licence. His P.A. had spelt my surname wrong, above the large, red Episcopal seal, but never mind; my surname has been spelt several ways: "Rae", "Ray", even "Wray"; and, this time, "Rui". You just can't get the staff...

So, here we are, after a long and hard journey. But, it isn't over yet; it is just beginning.

I feel that God is calling me to do a mission in September, in the Calasparra area. There are many Brits here who don't do church, yet I feel that a good deal of them are Christians.

I reflect long and hard on why people don't like churches, and I accept that one does not have to enter a building to worship God. He is around on Sunday morning walks, in the garden, or cooking over a hot stove. My problem is why sharing fellowship with other believers - which is so important - doesn't resonate with the majority; *Will I be expected to go every Sunday? What if I only want to go once a month, or now and again? I don't like some of the people who attend regularly...* Many questions and thoughts.

My feeling is that if the worship is sincere, and focused on the Trinity, then people who try a church will want to stay. It was once said that getting people over the threshold is hard work; losing them out of the back door is easy. In a small congregation, those who come and then don't are easy to spot - less so in larger churches. The key is to keep contact; not to let people disappear, without a friendly email, telephone call or even a visit.

*

The mission is taking shape.

In Norway I became involved in a tent mission, and had been invited to take part. Preaching inside a big tent was so different to churches: people came to find out about the Christian faith in a relaxed atmosphere.

I again recall my two questions, mentioned earlier – those which have stuck in my mind: "If you are about to have a car crash and shout *'Jesus!'* is it a prayer or a blasphemy?" And, the direct question: "Are you a pastor or an evangelist?"

At first, I didn't want to get involved. Time is precious, and I kept thinking that finding a room, musicians and song group would be a major problem. No matter how widely the mission is advertised, there is a strong possibility that no-one will come; waste of time and money. So, I kept pushing it to the back of my mind; the bottom of my "to do list" - a little like the decades I spent pushing away thoughts of ordination.

My experience is that if God wants something, He waits. He is outside of time. I had pretty much given up the mission idea, when in He comes again.

Jean and I had a similar thought, at about the same time: do a Gospel karaoke night. The Brits here love their bingo and quiz nights, and karaoke always tops the bill.

I had met a guy I call Disco Dave, who comes to my services when he is in Calasparra. He lives in the U.K. and has a house here - all the necessary professional equipment is at his home in Calasparra, plus masses of music. Dave's karaoke nights are very popular. When he did one, a couple of months ago, I got involved, and was able to show that I am a fun guy who can socialize, even when wearing my collar. My monthly magazine article, *The Rockin' Vicar*, circulates around Murcia, and the feedback is very positive. I try to show the human side of a clergyman, someone who has the same problems as everyone else, and understands life's difficulties.

I contacted a lady in our congregation, who knows Dave well, to ask for his contact details. Lo and behold, she replied that he was in Calasparra, but was going home the next day. I rang the number she gave me and arranged to meet him that afternoon.

We met at a bar, on the urbanization, where most Brits live or stay. I was rather apprehensive about Dave's reaction to my idea, but he was enthusiastic. He told me that he had been asked to do another karaoke evening, the previous Friday, with just two days' notice, and it had been a great success. He hadn't come to the chapel on this visit, because he was with a gang of mates from the U.K., and had spent his time enjoying their company.

I explained about doing a Gospel karaoke night, with Johnny Cash and Elvis Gospel songs, amongst others. We talked about having a slot in the middle, to quieten things down, and he asked if I know anyone who plays the guitar and sings. I knew two who would fit the bill, perfectly! We explored many possibilities, like me singing "Wild Thing", to The Troggs' backing, wearing a long wig (I have done this in churches, when explaining about John the Baptist), and Dave doing his Elvis impression.

The result of our get-together was that Dave would be in Calasparra in September, so we focused on Friday 13th, to much amusement. I immediately had a word with the owner of the bar and booked the night. He knows me, as I held services in a room there, before the chapel was built. If the people won't come to you, meet them where they are. I seem to remember reading somewhere about a Man who went out amongst the people...

I am also a drummer. In the U.K., Jean bought me a set of Premier drums, and I played in a song group, in a Blackpool church. Jean tried guitar, but we had to have her air-strumming during services, on an unplugged electric guitar, as she couldn't master the necessary chords. The drums have sat in the corner of my study in Spain, as I have not had the time to practice. Perhaps now is the time to rock again! My study is next to the garage, and there are no neighbours near enough to complain, so I can play to my heart's content, to backing C.D.s. It will be therapeutic! Maybe He has a plan for my drums, too…

As I say in my monthly articles, and to anyone who is feeling down: "Rock on!"

Hopefully, the retreat will be visited regularly and word will get around. So many are seeking peace and quiet in their busy lives, and precious time to relax and reflect. And, to pray; to be alone or talk confidentially, if and when they wish. Jean is a prayer counsellor. And, me? Well it, can be said that I have a fair old experience of life to share. And ministry.

Do have a look at the retreat website. If you would like more information or to stay, please do contact us: www.olive-grove-retreat.com.

ADDENDUM

A Funny Thing Happened on the Way to the Forum

I am always late going to bed - usually around 2 a.m. - and I check my emails and other social media, before departing to the land of dreams, or otherwise.

At about 12.30 a.m., on Sunday, I saw a message on Messenger, which blew my mind. It was from a guy called Sebastian, in Mar del Plata, Argentina, asking if I was the same Andrew Rea who spent some time in Neuquen. His mother Alicia was staying with him, and wanted to get in touch. My mind raced.

In my Argentina encounters I mentioned Cacho – the man to whom, with his business partner, I had lent money and flown from Neuquen to Buenos Aires, so they could buy building materials. The same Cacho who, with his wife, Alicia, taught me how to check if spaghetti is cooked, by throwing it against the kitchen tiles - forty years ago.

I opened the message and answered: "Si, soy Andrew Rea."

There followed an exchange of happy messages, during which Sebastian asked if I use Whatsapp, which I do.

On Sunday afternoon, after returning from my service in the chapel, I spent several joyful hours receiving voice messages from Alicia. We exchanged family news and photographs. Sadly, Cacho had died from a heart attack, a few years ago, and she had now moved from Neuquen to Mar del Plata, to be with her family. I saw a photograph of her daughter, Jesica, who had played with my own daughter; they were the same age and went to school together.

What goes around comes around! A lady I have not seen for forty years, and only knew briefly, took the trouble to find me, on the other side of the world. The exchange was very emotional, for both of us.

When I eventually got to bed, in the early hours of Sunday morning, I lay thinking about my Argentina experiences: the people; the crazy situations...

When I flew to Buenos Aires, with Cacho and his partner, the 'plane got caught in a bad storm, dropping thousands of feet, in seconds. I thought at the time that it was my punishment, for using missionary funds on a reckless illicit venture. But, we survived.

I have survived.

We all survive, I guess, one way or another...

AUTHOR'S ACKNOWLEDGEMENTS

As an ordained Anglican priest who relates my journey through faith and churches in four countries, England, Norway, Argentina and now Spain.

Through my early life, my work as a probation officer and in child protection, as a lay minister and coming to ordination late in life, I asked many questions about churches and tell how I have struggled to understand whether organized religion nurtures or stifles the Christian message.

I would like to acknowledge two Anglican bishops stand out in my mind with deep gratitude and respect. Nicholas Reade who ordained me in England and Carlos Lopez Lozano who welcomed me in Spain. Without their guidance my ministry may not have survived.

ABOUT THE PUBLISHER

Established in 2013 L.R. Price Publications has quickly established itself as one of the leading independent publishing houses in London, truly committed to publishing books by unknown authors.

We use a mix of traditional publishing methods with the latest technology and funding options to bring our authors' words to the wider world.

If you are an author interested in getting your book published, or a book retailer interested in selling our books, please contact us:

L.R. Price Publications Ltd.
27 Old Gloucester Street,
London, WC1N 3AX.
Tel: 020 3051 9572
publishing@lrprice.com
www.lrpricepublications.com

Andrew H Rea

HOLY INADEQUATE

Printed in Dunstable, United Kingdom